Skelton Kuppord, W Rainey

The Uncharted Island

Skelton Kuppord, W Rainey

The Uncharted Island

ISBN/EAN: 9783744725750

Printed in Europe, USA, Canada, Australia, Japan

Cover: Foto ©ninafisch / pixelio.de

More available books at **www.hansebooks.com**

THE
UNCHARTED ISLAND

BY

SKELTON KUPPORD

*Author of "Hammond's Hard Lines," "The Mess that Jack Made,"
&c. &c.*

THOMAS NELSON AND SONS
London, Edinburgh, and New York

1899

CONTENTS.

I. A MEMORABLE GALLOP,	9
II. A MAP AND A MYSTERY,	30
III. APPRENTICE AND STOWAWAY,	49
IV. A TWO-LEGGED CHAMELEON,	72
V. A TALL YARN,	97
VI. AN OLD SEA-FIGHT,	119
VII. THE CAMPADDER TREASURE,	135
VIII. MR. GRIFFINS' OPINION,	152
IX. A COUNCIL OF COLONELS,	169
X. NEW LIGHT ON THE SUBJECT,	187
XI. UNCLE ROLAND RELENTS,	206
XII. THE PAINS OF TREASURE-HUNTING,	223
XIII. THE WEASELS JOIN IN,	245
XIV. BROWNJOHN RAGES—MARTIN WINKS,	265
XV. TONY'S EXPEDITION,	287
XVI. THE STRUGGLE WITH BOX NO. 4,	303
XVII. LAW AND JUSTICE,	321
XVIII. OLD HOOKEY EXPLAINS,	338

LIST OF ILLUSTRATIONS

BY

W. Rainey, R.J.

"TWO OF THE MEN CAME AFT, LEADING BETWEEN THEM A MISERABLE PIEBALD OBJECT,"	*Frontispiece.*
"HERE HOOKEY HELD UP THE IRON HOOK THAT TERMINATED HIS RIGHT ARM,"	117
MAP OF TREASURE ISLAND,	148
"IT WAS NOT TILL HE HAD RETURNED WITH THE BRANDY, AND HAD GIVEN TONY SOME, THAT HE HAD TIME TO LOOK AROUND,"	261
"DOWN CAME MR. BROWNJOHN'S CANE ON THE SENTINEL'S MID THIGH,"	268

THE UNCHARTED ISLAND.

CHAPTER I.

A MEMORABLE GALLOP.

A SCIENTIFIC man has proved that crows can count up to five, so it may not be too extravagant to suppose that they know the alphabet. At any rate, that is one way of explaining why a great black fellow, that was flapping his way across the Merliston meadows to lunch in Farmer Jargin's cornfield, seemed to be puzzled at what he saw on his way. In spite of the importance of his business in the field beyond, the crow broke through his rule, and made a complete circular sweep round the centre of the meadow—a waste of time which can only be accounted for by his wish to know what the Merliston people meant by putting two white capital letters—T and Y —in the middle of their three-acre recreation field.

One sweep seemed to satisfy him, for he flapped on his hungry way. Probably his experience in scarecrows had quickened his skill in detecting human beings under any disguise, and thus enabled him to resolve the two letters into two boys in white flannels lying flat on the grass.

Tony Wedgeworth lay with his arms close to his sides, his hands in his trouser pockets, and his legs as wide apart as comfort would permit. He was Y.

Ned Campadder played the part of T, by lying with his arms outstretched at right angles to his body, his head being at Tony's feet. Each rested his head upon the grass, and breathed into the inside of a straw hat that lay upon the face to protect it from the sun.

Some people, when they wish to talk secrets, look out for an out-of-the-way corner or some particularly dark room. The crow's friends knew better. Experience had taught them that at Merliston School walls have ears, and even in Merliston woods the Dryads seemed to be particularly inquisitive. But here, in the middle of the meadow, they could talk without fear of being overheard.

It may seem as if they were liable to be caught by any passer-by, for they could see nothing at that moment but the insides of their hats, with the words:

"Natchet and Co., Hatters, 54 High Street. Best London Make;" and even this limited view was sorely out of focus. But experience had taught them the fact—though poor Mr. Aikenson, the science master, had failed to teach them why—that with their heads on the ground they could hear even the gentlest footstep at a considerable distance.

So they could speak to each other in their ordinary tones without fear. Still, though they had skulked a rather enticing river expedition expressly to talk over a very serious matter, they did not appear to be making the most of their opportunity, for any passing crow or schoolmaster would have suspected them of nothing worse than lazily sleeping away time that might be better spent. They had come to talk, yet they had lain speechless for nearly half an hour. The fact is that repentance of the best kind is silent work, and Ned and Tony were busy repenting.

Their repentance was just a day old. This was Friday, and they repented that on yesterday's half-holiday they had gone to the Crossroads; for if they had not gone to the Crossroads, they would not have been tempted to dare each other to enter the bar of the Cross Keys.

No, no; it is not quite so bad as *that:* it only

ran to lemonade and raspberry wine (mixed). The very mention of this compound sets the adult teeth on edge; but not here did the juvenile repentance begin. They did not repent of their tipple; they rather relished the memory of it. Their only repentance was because the Cross Keys happened to be out of bounds, and because if they had not gone there they would not have been tempted to push on to Baringstoke-on-Bream.

Mathematicians, with their usual pig-headedness, will no doubt maintain that all space is divided into two parts—*in bounds* and *out of bounds*—and will deny that there can be any degrees of *out of bounds*. But any Merliston boy will tell you that Baringstoke-on-Bream is five times more out of bounds than the Cross Keys; and if you want proof, he will explain that the *pœna* is five times as big for the town as for the inn—unless, of course, you have gone into the inn, in which case, naturally, there is no more to be said.

Now we know that Ned and Tony had been in, which may account for the daring plan they formed on their way to the town. One may as well be hanged for a sheep as for a lamb. The Cross Keys was the lamb; Trebaggs was to play the part of sheep. They would go to him, hire a couple of horses, and have a gallop along the Lymingage Road. It was Ned who suggested the plan; it was Tony who had the money. This was the usual arrangement. Tony's father was dead, but his mother was not—and she was rich.

At that moment—that is, after the lemonade—their joint stock of money amounted to one pound and ninepence, of which Ned's share was fivepence. When they reached Trebaggs's there was some little trouble. The old fox knew that he was out of bounds, and that he ought not to hire out his horses to schoolboys. He told them so. They pressed him eagerly, which was exactly what he had expected.

"Of course I want to pleasure you, young gents," he said indulgently; "but it's a big risk breakin' school law in this way, to say nothin' o' the impossibility o' trustin' my two best hunters to boys like you—for all my hacks is out."

This completed the case. Eager before, the boys now became rabid. The chance of the two best hunters raised their hopes; the implied distrust of their horsemanship wounded their self-respect. Seven-and-six was the usual charge for two hours of a hack; but in consideration of the exceptional value of the mount in this case, the youth of the hirers, and the breach of school law, the fee was raised to ten shillings each. Perhaps it would have risen even higher, had not the wily horse-dealer first found out the full extent of his customers' resources.

By the time that the two hunters were brought round to the yard, Tony's bright sovereign had quitted his waistcoat pocket, and had found its way to the right-hand trouser pocket of Trebaggs.

"Now, young gents, as you vally your lives, don't try any cantrips wi' them thoroughbreds. Don't judge them by your cobs at home. They're so game that if you put them at the telegraph wires they'll at least *try* to get over 'em."

But the boys had no time to listen to advice. Clambering into the saddle with more agility than dignity, they had the stirrup straps shortened to suit their legs, and were soon trotting along the Lymingage Road. This was the bit that they found it hard to repent of. When they remembered how the horses had fallen into a gallop, and had skimmed along that road like four-legged swallows, repentance seemed out of the question. At the bottom of their hearts the boys felt that they would do it again if they had the chance.

But what followed made repentance easier. After

a while they tired of plain trotting and galloping along the road. A convenient lane on the left tempted them, and as they turned down it another temptation assailed them, in the shape of an open gate into a field of grass. This field was separated from another by a low hawthorn hedge. The temptation proved too strong for Ned. Even the horses appeared to enjoy the fun of clearing it. Glancing around for something else to jump, Ned spied a long, low wall on the north of the field. The ground sloped to the wall, so the run towards it was brilliant; but just when he was preparing to lift the horse for the leap, he noticed that there was a little stream of water in front of the wall, which made the leap a much bigger affair than he had expected.

Here he lost his head. Had he pulled sharply up, he and his mount would have probably slipped ingloriously but safely into the stream, and escaped with a ducking. Had he given the beast free play, it was just possible that they might have cleared the obstacle; for, after all, the water was not wide. But he did neither. He half drew up, gave a warning shout to Tony, who was following—and then pulled himself out from among the turnips in the next field.

One never knows exactly how those things happen.

A moment ago you were in the saddle; now you are on the other side of the wall or hedge, kicking out your legs, and running your fingers over your ribs to get an idea of the extent of the damage. Ned was not long in discovering that he had suffered no serious injury, and in a twinkling was on the top of the wall. Here a ghastly sight met his eyes. The stream was running red with blood. The poor beast lay with his hind quarters in the water, and his head on the narrow strip of turf that skirted the foot of the wall. Blood was pouring from his nostrils; but the stream evidently owed its colour to other wounds, for a crimson stain kept welling up from the water itself. One fore leg was crossed over the other in a very unnatural way, and kept plashing irregularly in the water. A little beyond, Tony stood beside his horse, and gaped in horror. It was some moments before Tony could gasp out anything, and then it was only the cheerless words,—

"He's done for, Ned."

While he quite shared this view, Ned felt that something must be done. In all their escapades he was the natural leader, just as Tony was the natural paymaster. But a very few minutes were enough to show that nothing effective could be done. It was in vain that Ned clambered down into the water, and standing in the crimson stream tried to induce the beast to rise. The animal only blinked his glazing eyes, and gave out sounds that neither of the boys had ever heard from a horse before—sounds that they are never likely to forget.

"It's no good," cried Ned, in despair. "You mount and ride like the wind for old Trebaggs. Tell him to bring a vet."

Two things showed how unhinged Tony had become by this awful calamity: first, he mounted and rode off without asking whether Ned was hurt; secondly, when he came to the hedge he did not try to clear it, but went tamely round to the gate, which he dismounted to open. Once upon the road not a moment was lost, as the panting sides and steaming hide of his horse proved when the boy drew up at Trebaggs's place.

"Down!" cried the infuriated Trebaggs, when he had gathered some sense from Tony's panting words—"Sultan down! the pride of my stable! Are his knees much hurt, young man?"

"It's worse than that, I'm afraid," stammered Tony. "But come at once, and bring a doctor with you."

"Is the boy hurt?" cried the posting-master, with

a sudden change of manner that a careful observer would not have passed unnoticed. But Tony was not a careful observer, so he hastened to reply,—

"Oh no, he isn't hurt; at least"—for here Tony reflected that he had made no inquiries on this subject—"he didn't say he was hurt."

"Did he get up after he was thrown?" asked Trebaggs abruptly.

"Oh yes, and tried to get the horse to rise, but he couldn't."

"Who couldn't, you jackass? can't you speak sense?"

"Ned couldn't," was the bewildered reply.

With great self-restraint Trebaggs asked, with an appearance of extraordinary calmness,—

"Who couldn't rise—the boy, or the horse?"

"The horse," answered Tony sullenly, "and you'd better bring a vet."

"Oh, I'd better bring a vet indeed!" snarled Trebaggs, recovering all his recent ill-humour; "I'm not a good enough vet myself, I daresay!"

In a few minutes a dog-cart was brought round, and Tony was ordered to jump in. No sooner had he taken his seat than a hostler handed up a rifle, and as Tony looked in surprise towards Trebaggs, the latter growled,—

A MEMORABLE GALLOP.

"Take it, you idiot; it won't bite you. I can't drive and hold that too."

They had gone a considerable distance along the Lymingage Road before Tony mustered up courage to ask,—

"Is it loaded?"

"Is it your grandmother!" growled Trebaggs, evidently too much upset by the calamity to think of anything else. Then, as if reconsidering his decision, he snapped out,—

"No, she isn't loaded—yet."

Tony wanted very much to ask when and why she would be loaded, but he saw that this was an occasion to hold his peace. Besides, they would soon be there, and after all he had a gruesome suspicion of the probable use of the gun.

Coming to the first gate the boys had ridden through, Trebaggs got down, led his horse into the field, and tying him to the gate-post hurried with Tony to the scene of the disaster. Without paying the slightest attention to Ned, who was standing by in a state of abject misery, he stepped into the water and examined Sultan, who continued to quiver and give out those sounds that turned Ned's blood cold. A very brief examination was enough.

Turning towards Tony he took the rifle, and stepping back a few paces, still in the water, he pulled out a ball-cartridge, snapped it into its place, and taking deliberate aim at Sultan's head, fired. There was still some motion, but whether caused by the running water or by some lingering life was not clear. Trebaggs made sure by expending another ball. Then he turned to the boys.

"A fine day's work this, young men!" he said grimly. "There lies seventy-five pounds' worth of dead meat. Dear at the money, gentlemen, dear at the money."

It was certainly Ned's place to answer, but not a word would come. To the poor there is nothing more appalling than the mention in this reckless way of impossible sums. It was Tony who, remembering the twenty-pound pony his mother had bought him, ventured to remark,—

"Isn't that very dear for a horse?"

"Oh, you don't believe my word, don't you? Then I'll trouble you to come back with me, and I'll give you proof. Just wait with my trap till I get the farm folks to see about this carcass."

As the boys made for the dog-cart, Tony still carrying the rifle, neither uttered a syllable: this thing was past words. But when Trebaggs came up they had to talk, and talk to some purpose. Both tried to get the back seat on the homeward drive, but Trebaggs insisted that Ned should sit beside him. He had something to say to him. Once the start was made the questioning began.

"What's your name?"

"Campadder."

"Well, Campadder, how much money have you got?"

"Fivepence."

A cloud settled on Trebaggs's brow.

"Don't try no chaff with me, young man. How much money have you at home in your little bank, eh?"

"I have no money and no bank; it's only kids that have banks like that."

"Oh, indeed!—And how much money have you, Mister What's-your-name?"

"My name's Wedgeworth," answered Tony, with as much dignity as he dared.

"And how much money have you, Wedgeworth?"

"Fourpence."

Again the scowl, this time with the contemptuous accompaniment,—

"Well, of all the paupers! Talk o' beggars on horseback! Ugh! I'm ashamed to be seen beside you."

More inquiries drew out the amount of the boys' pocket-money—one shilling per week.

"Two pound twelve a year each. Five pound between you." (In his calculations Trebaggs made no allowance for holidays.) "Why, it would take thirteen years to pay off your debt that way. *That* won't do."

After driving along for a little in silence, Trebaggs turned to Tony.

"Your father is the richest, isn't he?"

"Father's dead," muttered Tony.

"Ugh!" muttered Trebaggs disgustedly. Things seemed to be going entirely wrong.

"But mother's very rich," added Tony soothingly.

"Ah, that's more like," commented Mr. Trebaggs contentedly. "Well, you write to her to-night, and tell her—"

"But, Mr. Trebaggs," interrupted Ned, "it was I who killed the horse; Wedgeworth had nothing to do with it."

"Maybe you'll speak when you're spoken to," grunted Trebaggs. "This young gentleman hires two horses, an' pays his money like a man. One of them gets killed; it don't matter to me who killed it. You can pay your share to Wedgeworth afterwards if you like—that's none o' my business—but it's Wedgeworth that's responsible to me."

By this time they had reached Trebaggs's office, where the boys were commanded to enter. The old man began to rummage among the very dusty papers on a very long file, and by-and-by he exclaimed,—

"Here it is! Just look here, young gentlemen."

There, sure enough, well towards the bottom of the file, was a receipt for seventy-five pounds, being payment for the bay gelding Sultan.

"Maybe you'll have sense enough not to question my word again, young men," said the dealer, with what passed for dignity. "A paper like that in a court o' law is a most uncommon unpleasant thing for folks that question other folks' words."

It did not occur to the boys to look at the date at which Sultan had been bought. If they had, they would have been astonished to find that Sultan must have been considerably over a quarter of a century old. But, as a rule, boys do not notice such details, particularly when the man who shows the receipt keeps a large thumb exactly over the date.

Trebaggs took a long time to make up his mind about the final terms he would offer the boys. At last he gave his ultimatum. As it was an accident, and they were only boys after all, he would knock off fifteen pounds from the price, and he would give them ten days to pay the sixty pounds in. They could pay it half and half, or Tony could pay the whole, whichever suited them best. The important thing was that the money must be in his hands within the ten days, otherwise he would county court them.

"And you know what that means," he concluded, which was precisely what they did not know. But for that very reason their fear was the greater. They left the horse-dealer's office with one idea deeply rooted in their minds. Sixty pounds must be raised within ten days, or the end of the world had come so far as Edward Campadder and Anthony Wedgeworth were concerned.

Throughout the interview there had taken place a marked change in Mr. Trebaggs's policy. At first he had been almost resolute in determining to report the whole matter to the Rev. J. Scrabner, the head-master of Merliston School. By-and-by he seemed more inclined to spare the boys this additional worry, and at the end he actually went the length of making one of his men drive the boys to the nearest safe point to the school, so as to avoid suspicion by making them at least less late than they would otherwise be.

In spite of the drive, and though the open-handed Tony had tipped the man to the full extent of his final fourpence, the two boys were punished for exceeding their leave-time. Some people think that punishment is always unpleasant. That evening Ned and Tony actually enjoyed writing out their three hundred lines each. They felt that they deserved the punishment, and did not resent the *pœna*. Besides, it kept them from thinking of their awful plight. Above all, it put off the evil hour of writing home for that money—the most dreadful thing of all.

They had arranged that they would write the necessary home letter immediately after finishing the *pœna*. This may be why Ned, when he looked up from his Virgil after putting down the words, *Nares et spiritus oris*, and saw Tony still ploughing on, determined to finish the sentence at least, though *oris* finished the exact three hundred lines of the Fourth Georgic. Precisely the same thing was done by Tony when in his turn he reached *oris*. The performance was repeated two or three times, so that the form master was astonished to receive from each of the culprits next day a *pœna* that included the whole of the Fourth Georgic. Now this book contains exactly five hundred and sixty-six lines.

The master was certainly not more astonished than the boys themselves, though they had means of solving the mystery.

"Why did *you* go on writing?" demanded Tony indignantly.

"Because I didn't want to begin to write home," was the honest though somewhat shamefaced reply.

"Same here," was the laconic answer. "I say, Ned, is there any hurry to write to-night? Ten days is a long time. Let's put it off, and skulk away to the meadows to-morrow and talk it over. I don't know what to say in the letter; do you?"

All this was said very quickly and nervously, but it fell into very willing ears. The feebleness of the argument was lost in the eagerness to be convinced. Ned was even more unwilling to write than was Tony, so it was agreed that the matter should be thrashed out on the meadow next day.

And now they lay on the meadow, and there was small appearance of the thrashing out. Ned had said,—

"My father is as poor as a church mouse."

Tony's reply, which under other circumstances would have been regarded as vulgar brag, really showed more tact than one usually expects to find in a boy of fourteen.

"And my mother's beastly rich; she doesn't know what to do with it."

There was a long pause before the next remark. Again it was Tony's hat that gave out the muffled sound.

"You may say, 'What's sixty pounds to her?' Nothing, I tell you, and I'd write and get it out of her to-day or to-morrow night, if it weren't for Mr. Darvel."

"What's he got to do with it?" re-echoed from under Ned's hat.

"Oh, he's made the mater promise to let him know all my demands. He's our lawyer or something, and he's afraid I'm being spoiled—on a shilling a week."

Ned wanted to explain that this was a special case, and that Mr. Darvel himself would admit that money spent under present circumstances could hardly spoil anybody; but he felt that the whole burden of the sixty pounds should fall on himself, and he could not be so selfish as to argue merely for his own safety. For a while he contented himself with silence, and a vain attempt to focus at one time the words on the inside of his hat, "Natchet" and "High." Then he spoke.

"I say, Tony, if you can raise that sixty pounds just now, remember I shall repay it some day, when

—when "—he concluded lamely—' when I have made my fortune."

"Of course, Ned," was the cheery reply; "the only thing that troubles me is whether I should write to the mater or to Mr. Darvel."

Ned's face flushed crimson under his hat, and it was then that the twenty-five minutes' silence began during which the crow was unsettled on their account.

The silence had become almost unbearable once or twice already, but had become bearable again the moment either of the boys thought of speaking. It was just becoming once more intolerable, when both boys sat up abruptly. They had heard a step on the ground.

It was that of Mr. Carleton. He was on his way to his own house, on the other side of the meadow; but he was not following the footpath that his daily journeys had made for him, but was making directly for the two startled boys.

"What's he up to?" whispered Ned; "he's owlier than ever to-day. Whose funeral has he been at, I wonder?"

"Sultan's, maybe," replied Tony, with a cheerless humour.

No more was said till the master was close upon them. He certainly looked uncommonly depressed;

but his tones were sympathetic rather than lugubrious when he said,—

"Campadder, you are wanted in the head-master's room."

"Wedgeworth too, I suppose," gasped Ned, as he slowly got upon his legs.

"No," answered Mr. Carleton, in some surprise, looking keenly at the boys; "there was nothing said about Wedgeworth."

"All right, sir," replied Ned, with strained cheerfulness.—"Will you come as far as the gate, Tony?"

CHAPTER II.

A MAP AND A MYSTERY.

SCREWING his courage up to the knocking-point, Ned waited till a deep "Come in" authorized him to turn the handle, and enter what was commonly known among the boys as the "Chamber o' Horrors."

Prepared for the worst, he was astonished when Mr. Scrabner received him with an outstretched hand and the sympathetic words,—

"Well, my poor boy, this is very sad news that I have for you."

"Yes, sir," replied Ned, sadly enough, but determined to say nothing till he discovered how the land lay. Mr. Scrabner looked up quickly from the letter he held in his hand, and asked in some surprise,—

"How did you know about it?"

Staggered for a moment, Ned soon recovered himself enough to stammer,—

"Er—Mr. Carleton told me in the meadows."

" Did he ? "

Mr. Scrabner was evidently annoyed at something, but he mastered his feelings, and resuming his sympathetic tone, said,—

" It was terribly sudden, was it not ?—the end, I mean."

" Yes, sir, but it was better; it would have been cruel to let him live longer."

" Eh, what ? Eh—well, yes, I suppose you are right. But I was not aware that he suffered much; I thought it was quite unexpected."

" Oh yes, sir. Nobody could have suspected it till he dashed his head against the wall, sir."

" Dear me," muttered the master, referring to his letter, " and they tell me it was an aneurism in the aorta. Well, well, I suppose they are quite right to keep those family matters to themselves."

Then turning to Ned he said kindly,—

" I suppose you'll start for home at once. You can catch the 3.20."

" O Mr. Scrabner, is it so bad as that ? "

The tears stood in Ned's eyes, but it was not this that surprised the master. The tears he had expected; the remark he had not.

" Do you mean to say, Campadder, that you

propose to go on with your usual work in the face of such a calamity? it is unfilial."

"Yes, sir; but Mrs. Wedgeworth will pay some of it, and my father will pay as much as—"

"But he's dead, isn't he?" interposed the schoolmaster, in bewilderment.

"Yes, sir—I saw them shoot him; and the farm folks were to bury him, or else—"

"Can the shock have turned the boy's head?" thought the master. Then after an anxious pause, during which he examined the boy's face, he went on, "What do you mean by shooting him? Why should any one shoot him?"

"To put him out of pain. Besides his head being dashed in, his fore leg was broken, and something—"

The master's hand fell upon Ned's shoulder.

"My poor boy," he began again, "we are talking of different things. Have you had any word from home?"

"No, sir," stammered Ned, noticing for the first time that the letter in the master's hand was black at the edges; "is—is anything wrong?"

"Yes, my lad: your father— But perhaps you'd better read for yourself," and the master adjusted his cravat with great vigour as he handed Ned the letter.

The boy read it through quietly. His face could not get paler than it had been on his entrance, but the expression rapidly changed. From being haggard and twitching it became haggard and set.

"Does it mean that he is dead already?" asked Ned, in a scared tone. "Shall I never see him again?"

"Not in this life, my boy," answered the master softly; and then he said some of those things that suit such occasions, but Ned could not understand him. He knew, however, that he was being kindly treated; so he gripped his master's hand, and muttered,—

"Thank you, sir. Yes, sir, I'll catch the 3.20, thank you."

Stumbling along the corridor, Ned came into the hall, where Tony was anxiously awaiting him.

"What cheer, Ned?" he began encouragingly; but a glance at his friend's face changed his tone.

"I'm to catch the 3.20 train, Tony. Will you help me to pack up?"

"Expelled, by Jingo! And what about me? Where do I come in, old chap? You're not going to go alone, I can tell you."

"My father," began Ned—"my father—my father's dead."

Not another word was said of the unfortunate affair of the day before. Tony did everything for his friend—from packing his little portmanteau up to buying a ticket for Breamington *viâ* Sardon-super-Mare.

Tony's first act on getting home from the station after seeing his friend off was to write two letters—for he had resolved the doubt by writing to both his mother and Mr. Darvel—giving an account of the sad end of Sultan and the consequent money difficulty.

Tony felt much better that afternoon, but Ned had a wretched time of it. From Breamington he had driven in a hired gig along the coast to Arnwyke Abbey, in the south orchard room of which his father lay dead. Though the Campadders were poor now, they had not always been. For more than three hundred and fifty years they had held the abbey, which was not always the ruin that time had made it. Originally it had been four times its present size, as was shown by the crumbling masonry that marked out the lines of the old walls.

Mr. Campadder had died so suddenly that everybody wondered how his death came about; but their wonder about how he died was nothing compared with their wonder about how he lived. The home farm, and the two other farms that still remained of the old Arnwyke lands, were the only apparent means of support for the Campadder family; yet the late squire had managed to wear decent clothes, and to fare comfortably, if not sumptuously, every day. His wife, too, had dressed well, and certainly maintained her position with dignity. The two girls do not interest us here, but that did not prevent them from costing a great deal to educate at an expensive boarding-school; and everybody knows that you cannot keep a fellow like Ned at Merliston for nothing.

Nobody quite knew how the thing was done, for Mr. Campadder made no debts; but they were soon to get a pretty fair idea. Uncle Roland was at the bottom of it all.

Let there be no mistake about this Uncle Roland. He was no fairy-tale uncle, either in his good or in his bad points. He had despised his brother all through his life—this was, perhaps, a bad point; but he had kept him supplied in moderation with money—this may be reckoned a good point. Ned's father had been ashamed to have connection in any form with trade. Roland had gone into business as a mere lad, and had now gained quite a large fortune as a merchant and shipowner. The dead man had despised Roland, as a disgrace to the gentility of the Campadders; but he had been content to live on his bounty, all the same. Uncle Roland was content that this should be so.

I daresay you will be glad to let me skip lightly over the lugubrious details of the first day or two at home. We first begin to be interested on the morning after the funeral. Uncle Roland could not afford to spend any more time at Arnwyke, so he called Ned into the library to talk seriously with him.

"I don't see any good in your mooning away any more time at Merliston, Ned. I'm quite willing to keep you there for a while, and then send you to the university, if you like; but in that case I shall wash my hands of you. But if you care to enter our house, I shall send you at once to our branch in Hamburg to learn German business, and by-and-by you'll drop into a partnership. In the second case your fortune is made for you; in the first you must make it for yourself."

"I want to do something for the mater and the girls," was Ned's irresolute answer.

"Oh, *they're* all right. I wouldn't trouble myself seriously about them if I were you."

"But I want to rebuild our house. I am the heir now, and I don't want things to be for ever like this."

"If you mean the abbey here," went on Uncle Roland dryly, "that does not concern you. The house and farms belong to me—don't jump like that—your father sold them to me years ago."

"And we've been living like paupers in a stranger's house?"

"Not quite a stranger, you know," corrected Uncle Roland; "though I admit that I did not trouble you much with my presence."

"All the more reason why I should rebuild my family. I'd like to go to India, Uncle Roland; have you a branch there?"

"Yes; but what do you want to go there for? I daresay I could find a place for you, but what would be the good?"

"We are reading 'Warren Hastings' in school, and it says there that Hastings made up his mind when he was seven years old to recover the estate that belonged to his fathers, and be Hastings of Daylesford."

"So you have made up your mind to be Campadder of Arnwyke, eh?"

"Yes," muttered Ned, in that shamefaced way that Uncle Roland caused in most people he talked to.

"And you're going out to India to make your fortune like Warren Hastings, eh?"

"I'd like to," answered Ned as before.

"In that case you'd better go back to Merliston, and work ten times as hard at your books as you have ever done before."

Ned looked the astonishment he did not dare to express. Uncle Roland answered the look.

"You think school has nothing to do with India. Hastings got on very well there, but you remember he was a great student. He was so fond of his book that the very ploughmen in his village noticed it. And if you mean to walk in his footsteps, you have to pass one of the most severe examinations in the country."

Now examinations represented to Ned everything that was horrible. India was out of the question.

Pursuing his advantage, Uncle Roland went on,—

"Suppose you give up seeking to restore the fallen fortunes of our house, and try to make an honest living for yourself."

"I don't want to be a clerk in an office," replied Ned slowly, "and I'm no good at school, but I don't think I'm afraid of work. I think I'll go to sea."

Uncle Roland looked steadily at the boy for a moment, then shrugged his shoulders.

"Upon my soul, not a bad move. It will lick you into shape anyhow, and we may make something of you after all. Anything's better than mooning about in this sleepy hole."

"Will you help me to go to sea, uncle?"

"I won't help you, I'll send you. Let's see: which of our ships is in England just now?"

As he pulled out a notebook to refresh his memory, he was interrupted by his nephew blurting out,—

"I thought you meant the Royal Navy."

"Another mistake, my boy. More examinations, you know. You couldn't pass, unless your school reports are all libels. Never mind: in our service the apprentices wear blue jackets with brass buttons, just like the Royal Navy people, and a little gold braid round the cap too."

As he spoke he kept turning over leaves. After getting the place he wanted, he made some calculations, and turned to Ned with a satisfied air,—

"If you are ready to start from Glasgow in five

days, you can join the *Arica*—1,215 tons, Captain Fleming—on a trip round the world."

He did not say that the first part of the trip consisted in lugging a cargo of coal from Glasgow to Rio de Janeiro; and Ned, carried away by this sudden prospect of freedom, and for another reason, of which more by-and-by, eagerly closed with the offer.

As soon as this matter was settled, Ned found himself caught up in a whirlwind of preparations. It did his mother and sisters good to have to attend to him. They had no time to be miserable with so much to get ready; and no right to look miserable, for that would be unfair to Ned—at any rate that is what they thought.

One of the first things Ned did was to write to Tony, telling him of the important change, and asking if there was anything fresh about the calamity.

"I cannot pay my share out of my wages," he wrote, "at any rate till I am through with my apprenticeship." He did not have the courage to write that his wages were on the princely scale of five pounds for the first year, five pounds for the second year, seven pounds ten for the third year, seven pounds ten for the fourth year, or ten pounds if he did remarkably well. In the whole four years he would not make enough to pay even the half of the price of Sultan. Surely an odd way to go about making one's fortune.

But Ned had another string to his bow. He knew that Arnwyke Abbey was not to be restored on the wages of an admiral, much less of a master in the mercantile marine. But the abbey itself held out hopes. It had no real claims to a ghost. It is true that towards the end of last century the fisher folks of the village had done their best to raise the old pile to the dignity of a place on the list of the haunted houses of this island. But their efforts were in vain, as all selfish efforts ought to be; for the government cutters ruthlessly materialized the ghosts into very commonplace men and barrels, confiscating the latter and sending the former to very unpicturesque prisons.

But though the abbey had failed to make good its rank among the haunted, it was at least the unquestioned owner of a secret; no vulgar secret that everybody knew and scoffed at, but a genuinely highclass affair in the way of secrets, rising, in fact, to the dignity of an unsolved mystery.

What made it better, too, was that it was a masculine mystery, if I may use such a phrase; for it was one of the few mysteries in which no woman has had a hand—at least so far as anybody knows now. If there had ever been a woman in it, she had been long ago wiped out by the ink-eraser of time.

It was a mystery with a treasure in it; and as if this was not enough, there was an island in it too. The mystery was absolutely complete, except for a murder; and if there was no murder in it, there was the next best thing—a hurried decapitation by a duly certificated Tudor headsman.

It was not so wobbly as most mysteries are. It did not depend entirely upon words and traditions; it had come down to our times backed by documentary evidence. Ned's mystery had at least black and white to show for itself.

Among the family papers of the Campadders was a queer map, such as some ambitious schoolboy produces when under examination in Standard V. in a Board school. There was no mistake about the island. No one could doubt the fact that this was the island where the treasure was hidden; for if any one doubted, all that was necessary was to point to the spot marked in the clearest of rudimentary Latin, *Hic thesaurus est.*

This legible label was to be found at the head of

a creek in the north-east of the island. Everything was as clear and shipshape as the most exacting map-maker could demand. There was only one trifling omission. The map-man had forgotten to say where the island was. Armed with the map, the dullest map-reader could have walked straight to the treasure; but that little piece of sixteenth-century carelessness had raised the matter to the level of a mystery.

This problem—find the island—had begun by driving a worthy Tudor cutthroat to the verge of insanity; proceeded to involve certain Campadders in investigations conducted by the government, with the assistance, it is said, of the rack and other labour-saving appliances; and finally worried the lives and misapplied the energies of a whole picture gallery of Campadders, who now perpetually frowned from the walls of the abbey, but who were supposed to have a special frown for any one who mentioned the map in their presence.

The cause of all this worry was a certain Walter Campadder, who, for valuable secret service to Cromwell, had been rewarded with a grant of Arnwyke Abbey and lands. It was one of the smallest of the monasteries suppressed in 1536, but it turned out to be one of the wealthiest. Why it was so wealthy, and why Sir Walter found it convenient to conceal his treasure, must be left for Ned himself to tell at a more convenient place. What we are mainly interested in at present is that the map was all of the treasure that had come down to Ned's people. It had, indeed, turned out to be a bit of a curse to the family. From the days when the accession of Queen Bess had restored to the Campadders the power of hunting for their treasure, they spent time and wasted opportunities in the fruitless hunt for this golden island. Even those who did not hunt seemed to suffer from the evil influence of the hidden island. If they did not waste time in seeking it, they did in dreaming about it. Among them all, none had been a more thorough-going dreamer than Ned's father.

This probably accounts for Uncle Roland's strange conduct when Ned asked for the map. Had the boy got any encouragement, he had intended telling his uncle about the calamity, but the reception of his request for the map drove all else out of his head.

Probably Ned had some sort of legal claim to the map; but boys of Ned's age do not litigate with their uncles. As soon as Uncle Roland saw how the land lay, he guessed the meaning of his nephew's desire to go to sea, and determined to do all in his power to drive this silly treasure-hunting notion out of his head.

"You'll never make a sailor if you go about with that maggot in your head."

Ned's only reply was a respectful request for the map, resulting in a very emphatic refusal. As the discussion went on the uncle warmed to his work, and concluded by telling Ned that the map would be presented to the Archæological Museum at Sardon-super-Mare, as an exceptionally fine specimen of sixteenth-century map-drawing. It was in vain that Ned pleaded and remonstrated. His prayers only hastened matters. The map was posted that night.

Early next morning old Mr. Patterscriever, the curator of the Archæological Museum, was awakened by his old housekeeper, who said that a boy had called who would not go away till he had seen her master.

"Most extraordinary!" said the old man. "But I can't get up in the middle of the night like this. Send the boy up here—or—eh, stay, Mrs. Snidders, does the boy look wild, or—eh—safe?"

"Oh yes, sir; 'e's a uncommon nice boy, sir, on'y 'e *won't* go away."

Ned's first impression on being shown in was that he had never seen a more comical-looking old gentleman. His next was that this kindly old man would be certain to restore the map as soon as he knew how important it was. Little did the boy know the collector's greed.

As soon as he had told his errand, Ned saw how mistaken he had been.

"The Campadder map!" chuckled the old gentleman. "A genuine sixteenth-century map—what a treasure! And the tradition too! Sent by last night's post, did you say?—Hey, Mrs. Snidders!"

Then recovering his calmness, he pulled a cord that hung over his head as he lay; and when Mrs. Snidders appeared at the door, he called out,—

"Send up Susan with the letters, Mrs. Snidders—send her up at once; I've got the Campadder map!"

"But it's mine," put in Ned anxiously. "I'm my father's heir, and my uncle has no right to give away my things."

"Oh—ah—yes—oh yes. Your uncle's your guardian, isn't he, my boy?"

"I suppose he is," was the dogged reply, "but that does not give him the right to give away my things."

"Perhaps your father gave it to him before he died, and—"

Here the old gentleman seized the letter that he knew contained the map, and in his excitement paid no more attention to Ned for a few minutes.

The boy was not to be put off. He kept plying Mr. Patterscriever with questions and arguments to which the old gentleman could find no very satisfactory replies. All the same, he never for a moment thought of giving up his newly-found treasure. Most men who feel themselves so clearly in the wrong as he did at that moment would have lost their temper. Mr. Patterscriever only cudgelled his brains for some means of satisfying the boy without giving up this delightful piece of antiquity.

"Why are you so desperately set upon this map, my boy?" he asked mildly; "most lads at your age are interested in different things altogether. Is there nothing that I can give you instead? There are some very rare eggs in my collection in the cabinet downstairs; or is it postage-stamps, hey?"

It took Ned a little time to bring himself to confess to a stranger that he wanted to make still another Campadder treasure-seeker. Mr. Patterscriever smiled a contented smile. Now he had it.

"For your purpose, then, my lad, you do not require the map at all. An accurate copy is good enough for you. Now, I'll tell you what. I'll have it photographed. Williamson makes capital copies, and it'll be just as good for you as the original."

"But I leave for Glasgow to-morrow."

"Eh, that's sudden, my lad. But it can be done in time. Williamson can do it. Or if he cannot, we can easily send it after you before your ship sails. The moment I get up—or I'll get up now," and the old gentleman made a motion that sent Ned to the door.

Mr. Patterscriever was as good as his word. Next day, before starting for the train at Sardon, Ned received a cardboard-covered packet labelled on the outside: "From J. Williamson and Co. Photographs only." He knew what it contained, so he did not open it, for at that moment he was full of grief at parting with so many people he loved—from his mother and sisters, through his old friend Briggs the coast-guardsman, down to Uncle Roland himself: for, after all, this business-like gentleman had more than half won the boy's heart.

CHAPTER III.

APPRENTICE AND STOWAWAY.

IN the inner pocket of Ned's jacket, keeping the photograph company, lay an extremely badly-written letter. Any of the masters at Merliston would have identified it at a hundred paces as the work of Tony Wedgeworth.

It began with a few words of sympathy about Ned's bereavement—words that were certainly culled from some book, or suggested by some master. The rest was Tony's own.

"It's a blue do about Sultan. Darvel won't let the mater stump up and the ten days is up in three days. This teaches me not to write to Darvel again, so I just wrote to the mater when you were going away and she let me go to see you off, and she sent me five pounds for my railway ticket but it dosent cost near that. So I'll see you at Glasgow at the

Cent Stat. Your train is in at 10.15 a.m. but I'll be in at 5 o'clock a.m. and I'll meet you when you come in. Aikenson looked up the Bradshaws for me. He says he wishes you were coming back.

"Cheer up about Sultan. *I have a plan.*—Yours truly,   Tony Wedgeworth."

Tony's plan kept Ned thinking all the way, but nothing came of his thoughts. If Mr. Darvel would not allow the money to be paid, and the ten days' grace expired the day after to-morrow, he could see no way of saving the situation. The only thing he was quite sure of was his own meanness in thus slinking off and leaving Tony to bear the whole brunt.

As the train steamed into the Central Station at Glasgow, Ned was hanging half out of his carriage window to catch a sight of his friend. But no sign of Tony could he find. It was only when he had got out, and was looking after his luggage, that he noticed a swarthy, black-eyed, black-haired, sailor-looking lad watching him with a grin. It was Tony.

"But where in the world did you get this rig-out?" cried Ned, admiring the dashing blue serge suit, the glittering buttons, and the resplendent thin gold band round the cap.

"Bought them in Argyle Street half an hour ago. Slops, you know. Aren't they a splendid fit—for slops?"

The concluding remark was called forth by the necessity of giving the right shoulder a twist, in order to fill up all the available space in the jacket at that spot. Unfortunately this twist seemed to disturb the balance of power between the legs, for the left trouser-leg at once dipped ominously near the ground.

"Well, you can't have everything—at any rate, not for two pounds seventeen and six, including the cap," apologized Tony, as he noticed the critical look in Ned's eyes.

"Two seventeen six!" cried Campadder, in dismay. "And you had only five pounds to start with."

"Yes; an' I've seventeen shillings left an' a copper or two," answered Tony, fingering the coins in his new pockets.

"But it costs you twenty-five and threepence to get back *third class!*"

"Well, I ain't goin' back, d'ye see? Didn't I say I had a plan?"

"And what's your plan?" stammered Ned. He felt pretty sure that the plan meant trouble for him, whatever else it might mean. Besides, the get-up of Tony suggested something.

Taking a tragic look around to make sure that he was not observed, Tony whispered,—

"I'm goin' to sail wi' you on board the jolly *Arica*."

"But I can't take you, Tony. You've no idea what a flint Uncle Roland is, and what a tartar Captain Fleming is. I'm sent to him because he's so hard. I—I really can't take you."

"'"Nobody axed you, sir," she said, "sir," she said,'" sang Tony contentedly. "I'm coming, all the same."

"Look here, Tony, don't be foolish about this thing. I'll get all the blame of it if you try on any of your larks. I haven't much money, but I've enough to make up your seventeen shillings into a ticket for home."

"Do you mean that, Ned?" asked Tony, with an odd glitter in his eye.

"Of course I do," was the eager reply.

"Then you're not the fellow I thought you,' said Tony slowly. "You grumble that I'll get you into a little trouble, and to save that you want me to go home and face old Trebaggs and his Sultan account."

"Tony, I—I forgot all about Sultan just now. I was only thinking of the awful tales Uncle Roland told me about Captain Fleming. Come on; I'm your man every time. If you're game, *I* won't flinch."

Tony looked doubtful for a moment, then gripped Ned's arm and cried,—

"Now for the saucy *Arica!*"

Again Ned looked troubled, and Tony suspicious.

"Well, what's up now?" This from Tony.

"It's your togs," was the reply. "Don't you see that if you come on board with that uniform they'll smell a rat at once, and your plan is done for. You must come in your ordinary clothes; the others can be brought out in a day or two."

"I believe you're jealous of my suit," cried Tony, complacently running his eye down his new garments. "Yours aren't a patch on them, you know. But anything to oblige a friend. Eh, I say, where am I to do it?"

"You couldn't manage in the cab, could you?" asked Ned nervously.

"What's to hinder, if it isn't a hansom? Isn't a growler dismal enough for the darkest deeds?"

But the Central Station proved to be too near the docks to give time for Tony's full performance. The cab drew up in Clyde Street, outside of Berth 37CA, inside of which the *Arica* was lying, before Tony was half done. But, after all, a pair of blue trousers does not look particularly nautical when surmounted by a tweed jacket and a bowler hat.

Tony's bag had to be got rid of before Ned would consent to allow him to enter the shed. The boys had to trust to the honesty of a ship-chandler on the north side of Clyde Street, and turn his shop into a temporary left-luggage office.

Within the shed what a disappointment awaited the two! By common consent they gazed at each other, and then moved quickly towards the stern of the vessel. There was no mistake, as they had hoped there would be. This overgrown three-masted coal-barge was duly labelled on the stern "*Arica*, Greenock."

The masts looked respectable enough, and the figurehead at the bow was decently clean; but everything else was inch deep in grime. The river itself was of the filthiest, appearing to be made up of equal parts of water, mud, and common corks—the kind that come out of black bottles. All the men who were standing about appeared to be in uniform—of a sort. At any rate, they were all dressed alike: a pair of coal-blacked trousers, a coal-blacked shirt open at the throat, a coal-blacked pair of braces, and an oily cap, reduced them all to a common level of indistinguishability. Their features were raised to a sort of G.C.M. of coaliness. The fondest mother could not have picked out her son among the crowd.

The deck was covered with a black oily substance that looked like mud, but was really a sort of fluid coal. When the two boys had clambered up a broad iron-bound gangway with no rail, they came to close quarters with this essence of coal that smeared the decks. They found it almost impossible to lift their feet, the leather of the soles of their boots playing the part of suckers, and fixing their feet to the deck. It was easier to skate than to walk.

While they were experimenting with this new coal compound, Ned saw two coal-coated figures dressed exactly like all the others, but which from their size he guessed to belong to boys, approaching. One of them, looking at neither Ned nor Tony, but very impartially exactly between them, asked,—

"Are you the new apprentice?"

Ned claimed the title, and introduced Tony as his friend.

"I'm to take *you* to the cap'n, when you come aboard."

Ned followed his guide, while Tony was left irresolutely gazing at the remaining grimy boy.

"D'ye suppose ye'll know me again?" grinned the black one. Tony was pretty sure he would not. What he had been thinking about was the extreme likeness between the two blackamoors. Wishing to be sarcastic in his turn, he remarked,—

"I thought you were off for a trip round the world."

"Well, I guess that's about the size of it. And what then?"

"Oh, I was only wondering how you expect to do it in this old coal-tub."

"You keep a civil tongue in your head, young man, though you *are* a friend o' the owners. Another word against the *Arica*, an' ye'll know the taste o' bilge-water."

Tony knew by the look of the white of the black boy's eye that any remark at that moment would be inopportune. He advanced to the outer bulwark, and admired the filthy Clyde water.

Meanwhile Ned had been brought before Captain Fleming in the cabin. He was a man with a face like a jargonelle pear and a voice like that of a corn-craik. His most ardent admirers could not maintain that he was plain; he was distinctly, positively, aggressively ugly. His body was short and squat, very broad, but obviously very strong. At that moment Ned saw him at his very best, so far as looks go—his legs were out of sight below the table.

He was just then in a particularly bad temper, for which perhaps he had some cause. A captain may be pardoned for getting angry when on the eve of sailing he gets word that his first officer, after having been trained to his ways, has been superseded by a total stranger. But Captain Fleming would have been angrier still had he known the sort of man his new officer was. Fleming hated most kinds of men, but the kind he hated most of all was the scholarly kind. Now Mr. Griffins, whose name had been just entered as first officer of the *Arica*, was one of the most scholarly men in the mercantile marine. He held a master's certificate, with certain trimmings in the way of extra honours; but he was only twenty-four, and was not old enough to get command of a large vessel. He owed his present appointment to his character for seamanship. Uncle Roland wanted Ned to be under Fleming so as to get licked into shape, but at the same time he wanted him to be under the influence of a well-trained man like Mr. Griffins.

Fleming did not know why the new man was sent, for Uncle Roland had not the habit of explaining all his actions; but the captain did happen to know that the new man held a higher certificate than his own, and he did not like that. He disliked all those theoretical fellows, and Griffins was uncommonly fond of theories.

"So you're Edward Campadder," croaked the captain, with less malevolence in his tone than Ned had expected. "Shake hands, my lad. Now, you do your duty, an' the *Arica*'ll make a man o' you. There's no good threatenin' you till you do mischief.—Wallace, you take him over to the office to sign his papers."

As the two lads left the cabin, Ned turned to Wallace, and said,—

"I say, I know where the office is; you don't trouble to come."

For this Ned had two reasons. He wanted to have a quiet talk with Tony, and, if the truth must be told, he was ashamed to be seen in the street with this filthy fellow.

"Ye may know the office, but ye don't know the cap'n if ye think I won't see you where I'm told to see you. We obey orders aboard the *Arica* as a general thing—*I* tell you."

By this time they had reached the deck-house, between the mainmast and the mizzen. Here Wallace bustled in, telling Ned that he would be ready in a few minutes. Creeping over to where Tony stood, Ned said apologetically,—

"It can't be always like this. Wait till you see the decks cleared up and washed, and the blue sky—"

"It's the apprentices that clean the decks, isn't it?" asked Tony grimly. "But never mind; *that* job'll be done before I come out of my hole. By-the-bye, where is that hole to be?"

Ned resented this throwing of all the responsibility upon him, as if Tony did not know as much about the *Arica* as he. But he could not openly complain; he felt so much in need of consolation himself that he tried to console Tony.

"I wish it had been anything but coal. I don't see how you're to live three days down that hole."

The two boys were peering down into the blackness of the hold.

"And what was it old Aikenson used to tell us about spontaneous combustion on board ships?" asked Tony, with a vague remembrance of one of the science master's lessons.

"Oh, I think that was only on the old-fashioned ships," replied Ned cheerily. "All the new ones are properly ventilated, and the gases are led off by pipes."

"I say, Ned, whether would you be spontaneously combusted, or choked with coal-gas?"

"It isn't so bad as that, it isn't really," began Ned irresolutely; "but we must see what Wallace has to say about it."

They went back to the bulwark, and glowered gloomily into the water, till a cheery hail from behind roused them. It was not till Wallace spoke that Ned recognized in the smartly-dressed naval officer the grimy Wallace of a few moments before. The only trace of his former estate was a certain blackness about the eyes and the finger-nails.

On the way to the office they learned all that was worth knowing about Wallace. He was finishing his apprenticeship. His time would be up in seven months, and he was jolly glad. Life was not all beer and skittles on board the *Arica*; as a matter of fact, they got beer only on Sundays in the deck-house.

"Where do you sleep?" asked Tony anxiously.

"In the deck-house, o' course."

"And where do you dine?"

"Dine—dine? Oh, I see. We grub it in the deck-house, an' Martin bosses the show."

"Who's Martin?" It was Ned who put this question.

"He's the third mate. Only apprentice like myself; but he's mate, an' we must call him 'mister.'"

"And has Mr. Martin any authority over you?"

"He isn't Mr. Martin, only 'mister;' you only call the second mate Mr. Anybody. Martin's plain 'mister.'"

"How many mess it in the deck-house?"

"Five: there's me an' Treevers, an' Scatlan an'—Campadder."

"So there are five bunks in that little shanty?"

"Six," corrected Wallace—"two on each side, one opposite the door, and one against the iron bulkhead. An' I'll thank you to speak o' the deck-house wi' respect; it's no shanty."

"Then there's room for another in your deck-house?" put in Tony.

"See here, youngster, I've thought that was your lay since ever I clapped eyes on you. If you take my advice, you won't. I tell you, you don't know the old man."

Ned looked reproachfully at his friend for thus foolishly giving away his plan; but Tony went on,—

"Well, since you know what I'm up to, maybe you'll give me a hint. What's the best place to stowaway in—in a coal-boat, I mean?"

"Stowaway! I thought you meant to pay your premium like a man. Stowaway, you young blackguard! Do you know that Fleming has never had a stowaway in his life? He brags about it every time he gets the chance of dragging it in. Anybody who knows Fleming would as soon think o' sneaking into Newgate at the tail o' Black Maria as o' stowawaying on board the *Arica*."

At this point they reached the office, where the two who had business to do entered, while Tony loafed about, turning over in his mind Wallace's dispiriting words.

Ned's business did not take long to transact. A clerk showed him a big double sheet of light-blue paper. In most indenture papers there is a big, handsome red stamp up in the corner, bearing the important word "Sixpence;" but sailors are not called upon to pay this tax. There was a good deal about the *Arica*, and wages, and instruction, and other things. The clerk showed Wallace where to sign as witness after Ned had affixed his name, and the thing was done.

"And now you've done it, aren't you sorry?" asked Wallace, with a grin.

As this did not seem a question that demanded an

answer, Ned kept silent, and that gave Tony a chance to return to the attack.

"I've been thinking that I'd like to spoil Captain Fleming's record. It's a pity that he should go all through life without one single stowaway. I really think I must oblige him. You won't spoil sport, will you, Wallace?—my name's Wedgeworth."

"Oh, *I* never spoil sport. But you'll remember that I gave you fair warning."

"Never fear; I can bear my own whackings—eh, Ned? We've had a not bad training in that way. Now, tell me squarely, can a man be safely stowed away among coals?"

"Oh, as to that, it's as easy as winking. In fact, coals is the best cargo going for stowawaying. It's not the coals you've to be afraid of; it's—"

"Oh, I'm not worrying about that," interrupted Tony flippantly; "what worries me is that abominable black hole. Is there air enough down that horrible pit—and don't they fasten down the hatches before they leave port?"

"You won't go into the hold, you gossoon. 'Tween-decks is filled wi' coals, but the ship's brought to the line before the 'tween-decks is quite filled. There's a good three and a half feet between the top o' the coals an' the upper deck. Ye can lie as comfortable's in a cradle on the top, if we tip you an old sack or two."

"But when the ship pitches, won't the coals go rattling backwards and forwards? and one of the lumps might hit me on the head, and turn my cradle into a coffin."

"Oh, my eye, you *are* a green one for a stowawayer. You don't think the coals get it all their own way like that! They're all divided up into lots by partin' boards an' the iron standards. The lumps don't wander much, I assure you."

Thus far Wallace had been led away by mere love of mischief. He knew that once the voyage had begun things would be intensely dull, and the prospect of the natural excitement on the appearance of the stowaway was something to look forward to. Besides, he had a half-shivering joy in picturing to himself the way old Fleming would carry on when he found that his life-long record was spoiled, and that his favourite boast was now rendered worthless for future use. Yet natural caution, and the knowledge that he was playing a terribly risky game, drove him to make some arrangements. It is true he felt that nothing very serious was likely to happen, since Tony was the friend of Ned, who was practically one of the owners.

There was no question of money; it was only a matter of sending on the premium to the next port. If Tony had been a common street boy, a genuine stowaway, things would have struck Wallace in a totally different light. As it was, however, he felt safe; but he did not neglect precautions.

"But, I say," he remarked, "aren't we goin' pretty fast? If I help you, my name must never be mentioned."

"Trust me for that," was Tony's careless answer; "we don't sneak, Ned and me."

There was that in his tone that carried conviction. Ned's manner, too, had its influence. Wallace entered into the plot.

Their arrangements were very simple. Tony was to take an affectionate farewell as soon as they reached the *Arica* again, and was to go off as if to the station. In reality he was to make all his preparations, and return to the *Arica* between one and two in the morning, when Wallace was to meet him and take him on board, in such a way as to avoid the old watchman who was responsible for the safety of the ship in the berth. If any one should be awake or any questions be asked, Tony was to pretend to be the new apprentice just arrived by the night train.

Reaching the *Arica*, the two boys were received by Martin, a happy young sailor who looked handsome in spite of all the dirt and grease with which he was covered. He invited Tony to stay for dinner. Tony accepted, and was sorry for it. Everything inside the deck-house was coal-dusty and clammy. Martin was dirty, and the two other boys were worse. In itself the dinner was good enough—broth, the beef out of which the broth had been made, and rice and jam. All the same, Tony ate little, and longed for the end of the meal. It did not last long, for there was much to be done on board the *Arica* that afternoon. Tony took the affectionate farewell they had agreed upon, and the boys separated, in order to spend the longest day that either of them had ever known.

Tony had the best of the time—at the beginning at any rate, for there is something very interesting in spending seventeen shillings on all manner of things likely to prove of most use in exceptional circumstances. Most of what he bought was edible, and was contained in tins. The interest began to wear off when he commenced to find himself unworkable. He could no longer carry all his purchases. Things indeed looked serious. It seemed, in fact, as if his only plan was to sneak up some entry, lay down his tins, and sit beside them keeping guard till it was time to make for the *Arica*. Fortunately, at this point he remembered the left-luggage office, and by tying together as many of his purchases as he could into bundles, he got quit of them all for a time for sixpence. This transaction reminded him of the bag he had left at the ship-chandler's. Hurrying back to the quay, he was just in time to redeem it before closing time. This proceeding cost him threepence, and the putting of the bag in the left-luggage office cost other twopence, leaving him with a beggarly sixpence for tea. The rest of the time lay before him, long, dark, and dreary, till the appointed hour.

It was indeed a weary wait. At first the shop windows and the people interested the boy; but by-and-by window after window was shuttered, and shopkeeper after shopkeeper padlocked their doors and went home. Tony envied them, and kept on walking. Finally the very grog-shops reluctantly closed their doors, and Tony felt himself indeed out in the cold. When the policemen began to go along the streets, trying all the doors to see whether they were properly locked, Tony thought it time to go to the station.

There he tried to get up some interest in the arrival

and departure of the late trains. It was nearly midnight when a long south train ran in, as if with the intention of breaking the monotony. If this were its intention, it succeeded perfectly. Tony's heart stood still, it is true, but his body moved with remarkable rapidity to the other side of the book-stall, for out of a first-class compartment had stepped none other than Mr. Darvel.

As soon as Tony's heart had gone down to its usual number of beats, he started to wonder what had brought this objectionable person to Glasgow at such an inopportune time.

"What a narrow squeak!" he muttered; "if he'd seen me, it was all up. He'd have wanted to know all about it, and—but where can he have gone to?"

Coming from his post behind the friendly book-stall, he asked one of the few porters if he had seen a gentleman answering to the description of Mr. Darvel.

"He's just arrived by the 11.38—it's twenty late—an' gone into th' 'otel there. You'll catch 'im if you go straight in."

The man persisted in leading him to the hotel door, which opens off the arrival platform. There was nothing for it. Tony had to enter, thinking of the spider and the fly all the way; but no sooner had he gone in by one door than he left by another, slipped round to the left-luggage office for his bag and his tins, and made for Berth 37CA at his best speed.

* * * * *

Just as the neighbouring clock rang out the appointed one o'clock, Wallace saw the fugitive appear at the appointed place at the stern. A plank had been placed there judiciously during the day by the thoughtful Wallace, who had selected that part of the vessel as the least liable to interruption. Nobody who knew anything about the *Arica* cared to disturb the slumbers of Captain Fleming, and those slumbers were conducted in the stern regions. But the runaway was so burdened with his tins that he could not face the plank till Wallace had come over and shared the burden.

Stealthily the two crept forward till the hatchway was reached. Everything was pitch dark; each step had to be carefully selected by trial. Instead of going down the usual wide entrance, they crawled down a vertical iron ladder at a sort of side inlet to the 'tween-decks. It was here that a little trouble arose. In the midst of the absolute stillness came a clatter that sounded loud enough to awaken the dead, to say nothing of a light-sleeping old watchman who ought not to have been asleep at all.

"What's that?" whispered Wallace, who was following the stowaway down the ladder.

"One o' the tins got off its moorings," was the muffled reply.

"Down you go, an' I'll up on deck to bluff any one who comes along."

The fugitive had the gruesome pleasure of listening to a subdued conversation between Wallace and the old watchman, who had his own suspicions as to the strange sounds. Fortunately his suspicions took an altogether false direction, which gave Wallace an opportunity of giving a very picturesque explanation with which the old man professed himself to be satisfied, when assisted to forgiveness by the gift of one of the offending tins—or rather by the promise of it; for Wallace, it is shameful to relate, did not keep his part of the bargain, and the watchman found it to his advantage not to press his claims.

In a few minutes Wallace had regained his ally without any loss of provender, and very soon had him comfortably hidden in a place he had contrived for him between certain well-built pieces of coal.

"You'll be all right on those flour-bags, old man; as soft's a feather bed. The coals can't tumble on you, however much she pitches; I know what I'm about. Good-night."

No answer coming, he said good-night again, and was moving off, when a faint question made him turn.

"Oh, as to that, we must do as things'll do wi' us. Campadder'll come for you when we're fairly off, an' out o' range o' your bein' sent home in a tug or landed on the Irish coast. I hope you're as sleepy as I am. So long."

CHAPTER IV.

A TWO-LEGGED CHAMELEON.

HAD Tony been able to view the deck of the *Arica* next morning as she left her moorings, he would not have recognized the filthy coal-barge in the tidy and well-washed vessel. All the coal was out of sight, and all trace of it had been completely removed from the upper regions. It had cost a day's work, in which Ned, and a particularly shabby swab that had been allocated to him, had taken quite a prominent part. But Tony had other things to think of that morning.

To Ned's surprise almost no sails were put up. Everything was left to a tiny little tug-boat, on the paddle-box of which was painted, in brilliant yellow letters, the name *Flying Foam*. It looked at first ridiculous, almost humiliating, that the huge *Arica* should be dependent on the midget of a tug; but when Ned found that the *Arica* was to be only one of three vessels which were to hang upon the little steamer's tail, his respect rose enormously for this puffing little *Flying Foam*.

At first it was very slow work, something like eight miles an hour; but by the time they had reached Greenock, the tug seemed to have warmed to her work, and progress became more rapid. When they had reached Ailsa Craig, Ned felt distinctly uncomfortable; when the *Arica* passed Loch Ryan, he could no longer conceal the fact—he was shamefully sea-sick.

Naturally he wished to hide his shame in the deckhouse, the nearest approach to a home that was left to him. But Treevers unfeelingly drove him forth, advising him to stick to leeward till he was fit company for decent folks. For more than an hour Ned hung on, or over, or under the bulwarks, as circumstances demanded. He was half dead when Martin was relieved from duty and came to pick him up and lead him to the deck-house. There he gave Ned some brandy, and Treevers a bit of his mind for inhumanity.

Ned had been billeted on the port side, as he was to be in the first mate's watch. Being the newest arrival, he had to content himself with the athwartships bunk, which had the disadvantage of having no porthole, and was therefore dark and stuffy. Under the present circumstances, however, it was the very best place for him. He had no one either above or below him, as he would have had in the more comfortable bunks. He could, therefore, lie in peace, and groan without annoying anybody very much. As a matter of fact, the proceedings of the *Arica* and her crew had small interest for him during the next three days. Sometimes the thought of Tony lying among the coals would rise in his mind, but it was soon dismissed. For if Tony were well enough, he had enough tins to keep him going for a fortnight; and if he were ill, it did not matter whether he lay on coals or in a bunk—he would never notice the difference. At any rate, that was how it struck Ned.

On the fourth day out, Wallace insisted that something should be done for the poor stowaway.

"I've been along this mornin', an' he says if you don't come he must come out himself. He's been as bad's you, an' is more than half dead. *I'm* not goin' near 'im again. I was nearly caught as it is, an' I'm goin' to run no more risks."

Pulling himself together, Ned tumbled out. Wallace soused him from a little bucket, and did all he could to stiffen him up.

"The old man's below just now, an' has had his dinner. This is your best time. Maybe he'll not be so turk after all." Then as Ned moved off, "Mind you, *I'm* not to appear in this affair. If I do—"

Ned did not wait for the completion of the threat, but shook himself free from the grasp of the senior apprentice, and stumbled along to the place he had been told on the first day was the captain's cabin. Knocking gently at the narrow door, Ned heard from within a sound not unlike that of distant thunder. Taking this for an invitation to come in, the boy turned the handle and entered. The room was much smaller than Mr. Scrabner's Chamber of Horrors at Merliston, but it deserved the name much better. Ned could see nothing but three bunks, a triangular table, and a cloud of smoke. Out of the cloud came the gruff words,—

"Well, what do you want?"

These were not all the words the captain used. Some words he liked I have had to leave out because I cannot spell them. But it is fortunate that this omission makes no difference in the sense.

"Captain Fleming," began Ned timidly, "I have come to tell you that there is a stowaway among the coals."

I regret that there is not a single word in the captain's reply that I can spell. Ned was horrified. He did not know what to say, and wished he were anywhere else in the whole world; even the Merliston Chamber of Horrors would have been a relief from this.

After a few more unspellable words from the captain, Ned understood that he was being asked how it was known that there was a stowaway. Ned's tongue refused to work for a moment or two. At last he gasped out,—

"I hid him among the coals."

More remarks from Fleming, to which Ned tried to reply; but the captain shut him up and rushed upon deck.

When Ned reached the deck, he found the captain storming at everybody, and ordering everybody to bring the wicked stowaway to him.

In a very few moments two of the men came aft, leading between them a miserable piebald object. For the flour from the bags and the dust from the coal had made a very peculiar mixture. What shocked Ned was the haggard face with the grimy streaks down it. Moisture of some kind, perhaps perspiration, had evidently been streaming down the face, and had mingled with the coal dust and the flour so as to make black and white streaks—a very zebra of a face.

But a bigger shock still resulted from a closer examination. In several places Tony's black hair appeared almost white. Ned had heard stories of men growing grey in a single night of agony. He had never quite believed them, but now his doubt was of small comfort. Besides, Tony had been more than three complete days and nights in that terrible coalhole. Ned was aroused out of an unhappy dream, in which he was trying to pacify Tony's raging mother, by the question, put in a stern tone,—

"Who are you?"

"Tony Wedgeworth."

Ned started at the sound. It no more resembled Tony's former voice than Captain Fleming resembled Mr. Scrabner.

"Where did you come from?"

"From Merliston School."

"Where is that?"

The stowaway named Breamington, as the place most likely to be known to the captain.

"Who helped you aboard?"

"Ned Campadder."

As he spoke, the stowaway turned appealingly to Ned, who gave a new start as he received a new shock. Tony's black eyes had turned to light grey.

"Oho! then you're a schoolmate o' Campadder's," growled the captain, in a tone of relief. "Your folks are well off, hey?"

"My mother's very rich, sir, but she wouldn't let me go to sea."

"Hum! I thought so. So you're no stowaway after all. Your premium will be paid all right.—Here, Wallace, you see him fixed up in the spare bunk in the deck-house;—and, mister, you will see that his name is entered on the books. I'll log him just now."

Turning away, the captain let his glance fall upon the astonished face of Campadder.

"Get out o' my sight," he cried fiercely, "you an' your croakings about stowaways."

Thanks to the captain's determination never to admit that he had ever harboured a stowaway, the affair had blown over much more easily than any one could have expected. Everybody was pleased—everybody but Ned. His head was still swimming; his brain refused to work properly. Was this Tony, or was it not? His hair, his eyes, his voice, were changed, and yet he knew all that only Tony could know. He was brought to his senses by Wallace's voice in his ear,—

"He ain't Tony Wedgeworth any more'n I am."

"How do you know? *I'm* not sure, and I've known him for years. He *has* changed."

"Rather! Tony Wedgeworth had a fine haw-haw English accent; this chap spells Glasgow in every word he says."

"His hair may have changed by the agony of his time among the coals, and—"

"An' everybody knows coals come from Glasgow, so they've given 'im the accent, eh?"

"At any rate, don't say anything yet," pleaded Ned.

"Me! it's none o' my business. Catch me bringing myself under the old man's claws."

As soon as Wallace turned away, Tony glided up to Ned, slipped a letter into his hand, and followed Martin, who had stood keenly watching the whole performance, but who did not seem to think of taking any notice of what he saw. Moving round to the lee of the deck-house, Ned tore open the envelope that had no name upon it, and to his astonishment exposed a letter in Tony's well-known handwriting. It was very short and in pencil.

"Dear Ned,—It's a blue do about the *Arica* too. Mr. Darvel is here. The mater told him where I was and he came here. She can't help telling him things, about the five pounds too. So he knew. And the bearer is a poor beggar and very hungry and wants to go to sea. I told him to say he was me and he will tell you all the rest. Write to me from Rio.—Yours truly, Tony Wedgeworth."

Here Ned paused to consider the whole matter. He could make nothing of it. Why had Tony sent this poor beggar instead of himself? There was nothing for it but to ask the new Tony. At the door of the deck-house Ned met Wallace bouncing out with horror in his eyes.

"He's dead, Campadder. What are we to do?"

"Who's dead?" was the natural if aggravating reply.

"This strange stowaway," panted Wallace. "Treevers and I were giving him a rub down, an' he dropped dead in our hands. We didn't hurt him. I mean he just dropped himself."

The other lads now raised the body and placed it on the table at the end of the deck-house.

"I say, Treevers," cried Wallace, who had now recovered some of his coolness, "off you go and try to get Martin quietly. Don't let anybody know. He'll help us if he can."

Wallace and Campadder gaped at each other helplessly. They were not so silly as the reader may suppose. They knew as well as others that the proper thing to do in such cases is to loosen the cravat and dash water in the face. But this was impossible under the circumstances, since the new boy was already stripped to the waist, and had been soused two or three times in cold water before he had dropped. As to brandy, they had had sense enough to give him that. But boys who get even beer only on Sundays do not usually have a large supply of brandy on hand for immediate use.

In desperation Wallace started to rub the cold sides of the body, but stopped immediately.

"O Campadder, just feel his ribs! He's more like a skeleton than a stowaway."

Ned shrank from touching the cold, damp body. But touching was not necessary; the leanness was plain enough to the eye.

As they gazed at each other, Martin came quietly into the deck-house. Going straight to his locker, he undid the padlock, and pulling out a flask, applied it at once to the prostrate boy's lips. He wasted no time in finding out whether the lad was dead or not. If he were dead, nothing mattered; if he were alive, brandy was the thing for him. So at least ran the young officer's simple medical rule. In this case it worked. In a few minutes the body quivered.

Then Martin made a mistake. All medicine is not simple. What's good for the inside is good for the outside, is a simple but not always safe rule. Rubbing the body with brandy seemed to cool it rather than warm it.

"When we had sore throats at Merliston, the pole-cat used to rub us with camphorated oil," said Ned.

Martin did not wait to find out that the pole-cat was the matron in Ned's school. The word "oil" was what struck him. The only available oil was lamp-oil, and the young officer, taking it for granted that the camphor did not matter much (in which, by the way, he was not far wrong), started a vigorous rubbing to a lamp-oil accompaniment. It may have been the brandy, it may have been the oil, it may have been the rubbing, it may even have been plain, unassisted nature; in any case, Tony opened his eyes. Then came more brandy, a little more rubbing, and finally a bundle up into the spare bunk, with a double dose of blankets. The under blankets suffered a good deal from the oil; but as Tony would have to attend to the washing of them himself by-and-by, nobody paid much heed to that.

"I'm hungry," groaned the patient.

"Hungry!" exclaimed Wallace; "why, the young glutton came aboard wi' a cargo o' tinned meat that kept his line below the easiest Board o' Trade level. I could ha' lived on his stores for a month."

"So you saw him come aboard?" queried Martin, with a quiet smile which let Wallace see too late that he had let the cat out of the bag.

The officer made for the door. Wallace laid his hand upon his arm.

"I hope you won't—"

"Pfff—" snuffed the mate; "that's none o' my business. I'm off to see if the cook can give me anything hot for him."

"Confound him and his tins, an' you an' Martin an' —an'—an' my own foolishness," growled Wallace, turning to Ned, who had hardly spoken since the third mate had entered. "The whole ship'll soon know I'd a hand in this business."

A very few minutes brought a steaming pannikin

of soup within range of Tony's hungry jaws, and in a few minutes more he was off in a healthy sleep.

An hour later Wallace and Treevers were discussing the strange events that had happened in the deck-house, and Wallace did not forget to mention the tinned meats that had only been spoken of in the absence of Treevers. Now Treevers was a plump little Yorkshireman, with a cheery disposition, an enormous appetite, and an accent and dialect that I dare not attempt to reproduce.

"I say, Wallace," he began, "if you'll keep my place here for a moment, you'll hear of something to your advantage."

After bickering a little, and finding that Treevers would not disclose his plan unless set free to work it out, Wallace consented.

In less than a quarter of an hour the little Yorkshireman was back with a large tin under each arm and a small one in each hand.

"Just as I thought," he cried gaily: "the poor beast had forgotten to bring a tin-opener, and must have lain there starving in the midst of plenty."

"How do you know he hadn't a tin-opener?"

"Common-sense," growled Treevers contemptuously, as he laid out his treasure on the deck. "Can you imagine a man starving with a big tin of "—here he scanned a label—"of roast turkey, another of Paysandu tongue, a little tin of salmon, and a little tin of—what in the world is it?"

The concluding remark was called forth by the dilapidated state of the tin. The label had been torn off, and the tin itself smashed into a very fantastic shape. The case had held tight, however, and not a drop of its contents had escaped.

"There's one big tin down there that from its shape I should say holds pancakes. He must have danced on it to flatten it out so. I'll get it by-and-by. Won't we have a proper tuck-in to-night, old boy!"

The tuck-in came off all right, and a merry time they had of it in the deck-house; though Ned had to be absent on duty, and Tony had to be content to take his share of his own tins in his bunk.

It was next morning before the impatient Camp-adder got an opportunity of a quiet chat with the boy who called himself (and whom we must continue to call) Tony Wedgeworth.

Standing to leeward, and supporting himself by his left hand resting on one of the ropes, the new boy looked quite handsome. The slops fitted him much better than they had the original owner. The frank face, with its honest grey eyes, made an excellent impression on Ned. From their position on deck it was impossible to be overheard, so Ned asked in his ordinary tones,—

"Now, Tony—I suppose I'd better call you Tony, to keep up the farce—are you going to tell me all about it?"

"Yes," answered Tony, in that book-English he always used when on his guard; "your friend told me to tell you all about it."

The boy having paused a moment, as if uncertain where to begin, Ned helped him out by asking bluntly:

"Who are you, anyway?"

It appeared that he was a certain Archie Campbell, whose father had died and had left him destitute. The story was long, and perhaps not very interesting. At any rate, it will save time if we tell it for him. Archie was not a very good story-teller, though he had gone through all the standards of a Board school.

Archie had begun life as a message-boy on four shillings a week, but had fallen into bad company, and had done something that cost him his place. Ned wanted very much to ask straight out what mischief the new Tony had been up to; but he remembered Sultan, and thought he had better attend to his own affairs.

Archie had gone from bad to worse in that easy way that leads to painful consequences. In his case it had led to rags and *dossing*. Ned was unacquainted with the verb *to doss*, so Archie had to explain that it meant sleeping out of doors—on doorsteps, under bridges, or in wharf-sheds, as in his own case. For in despair of getting another job, the boy had made up his mind that he would run off to sea. He had no hope of being taken on as a boy in the usual way, since he had no friends and no character. His only hope, then, lay in sneaking on board some promising ship.

On the night of Tony's escapade Archie happened to be dossing in Shed 37CA. The shed was empty, as the cargo had been disposed of on board the *Arica*. This made it all the more difficult to doss there; for one of the dosser's bugbears is the policeman, who makes the rounds of the sheds and wakes up and moves on all the sleepers he comes across, and it is so much more easy to keep out of sight in a full shed than in an empty. However, Archie had dodged the policeman, and had dropped into 37CA just after the official bull's-eye had run through the whole empty shed. A bundle of straw in a corner supplied an exceptionally comfortable bed. Archie lay down in great ease, for he did not expect a second visit from the bull's-eye that night; and if any one knew the habits of bull's-eyes, it was Archie Campbell.

He was, accordingly, very much surprised, a little after midnight, to hear a fumbling at the postern door in the great gate opening into Clyde Street, and by-and-by to see a boy enter stealthily. It was not dark in the shed, for the street lamps are so arranged that one half of each lamp is inside the wooden wall of the shed and the other on the outside, so as to light up both the shed and the street. It was, therefore, not difficult for the eyes of Archie, accustomed as they were to the dimness of the shed, to see that the new-comer was extremely anxious not to be observed. The natural result was that Archie set about thinking what advantage he could draw from the other's fears. Rapidly making up his mind, he advanced suddenly upon Tony, and called out boldly,—

"Hullo, you, where are you goin' wi' them tins?"

Tony gave a start that caused one of his bundles of tins to drop to the ground, but he soon recovered himself sufficiently to reply,—

"What's your business?"

"I'm the watcher of this shed," said Archie, in his best style, trying to bluff the new-comer.

But Tony was not so easily bluffed. Looking superciliously up and down Archie's rags, he sneered,—

"Get out; I ain't a crow! You can't scare me!"

Archie saw that a different line would pay better, so he confessed that he was starving, and pled for something out of one of the tins.

Tony good-naturedly enough opened a tin of sardines, not displeased to find company for the three-quarters of an hour he must yet wait. He was almost scared at the way in which his sardines were gobbled up.

"You *are* hungry," he remarked; "I think I can spare you another tin. Which is it to be this time? you can have your choice."

Without pausing to discuss the quality, Archie at once pounced upon the biggest tin; which, however, Tony felt compelled to bar.

"You can't eat more than one of the little ones, you greedy beggar; it'd go to your head. Which of the little ones is it to be?"

Archie chose plain beef, and while he was disposing of the entire tin, Tony had time and inclination to tell of his own plans. He varied his story by asking all manner of questions, which Archie seemed in an excellent position to answer. They bore largely on the duties of apprentices on board vessels like the *Arica*, and had a constant reference to the amount of cleaning that fell to their lot. The answers were not at all to his liking, if we may judge by his exclamation,—

"I wish I were jolly well out of it. There's a jolly deal too much of the housemaid about all this!"

The two boys were already very friendly. Tony was busy explaining that he had no objection to give another tin, but that really Archie must promise not to open it till to-morrow, unless he wanted to explode, when they were both reduced to silence by a sound at the postern gate by which Tony had entered. With two tins inside him, Archie was no longer the timid dosser of a few minutes ago. All the same, he did not want to get into trouble. Besides, he was unwilling that the tin-giver should suffer. He accordingly pulled Tony swiftly over to the heap of straw, where the two were in a twinkling out of sight.

Peering through the friendly straw, the boys saw

a well-dressed gentleman enter by the postern gate, followed immediately by the policeman whose bull's-eye had been successfully dodged by Archie at an earlier stage. His name is immaterial, but it will be convenient to speak of him by the label on his collar, R36. The two would certainly have heard the rustle of our disappearing friends had they not themselves been talking as they entered.

"It's quicker this way than round the end of the shed," said R36.

As he spoke, the policeman, from force of habit, swept his bull's-eye round the shed. The light came to a natural stop on the flaming red label of one of the tins; for in their flight the unfortunates had left their provisions behind them.

"Hullo, what's this?" cried R36.

Mr. Darvel—for the reader has no doubt been as quick as Tony in recognizing the gentleman—went forward, and kicking one of the tins, remarked,—

"It looks as if some one was making provision for a voyage. I shouldn't wonder if my friend Tony were not just very far off from those concerns. He likes good feeding, does Tony."

With that they began to search the shed, beginning, very naturally, with the heap of straw. It may be difficult to find a needle in a haystack, but it is remarkably easy to find a couple of boys in a bundle of straw.

"Come now, Tony," said Mr. Darvel sarcastically, as the two lads stood sheepishly before their captors; "really I thought you might have said good-bye to *me*. Of course I never expected you to think of your mother; but a tender-hearted fellow like me! I might have died of a broken heart, you know."

Tony said nothing. He looked exceedingly black, but under it all I am not sure that he was not glad to be compelled to give up the housemaid's work on board the *Arica*.

"Are you going to come home quietly?" asked Mr. Darvel; "or shall I ask the help of this gentleman?" turning to R36.

"I'll come all right," said Tony; "but I must write to Ned. You'll let me write to Ned, won't you?"

"By all means, admiral," replied Mr. Darvel; "but I don't carry about writing materials with me at midnight."

"It'll be too late in the morning; the tide serves at five o'clock."

Here R36 suggested that he could get a piece of paper and an envelope from the weighing-machine box, that was open all night. While the policeman was off on his errand, Mr. Darvel turned to Tony.

"While you're writing to Campadder, you may as well tell him that we've settled the horse business."

"What have you done about it?" asked the boy, quivering with excitement.

"Don't worry about that affair, my lad. It was all a big swindle. Sultan was an old, worn-out beast, that should have been shot years ago. No doubt he had been an excellent thing in horse-flesh in his day, and his end shows that he had far more spirit than strength; but as for money, he was worth just what his poor old carcass would bring."

It appeared that Trebaggs had depended on the boys keeping it quiet, and only telling Tony's mother, who knew nothing about horse-flesh. But Mr. Darvel's appearance on the scene had put quite a different aspect on everything. Afraid lest the story should damage his legitimate business, Trebaggs had been extremely glad to say no more about Sultan and the sixty pounds.

It was this Sultan business, however, that had roused Mr. Darvel's suspicions about Tony's intentions, and had driven him to make a personal appearance on the scene. Putting one thing against another,

Tony could not honestly say he was sorry at the way things had gone.

When R36 returned, with a yellow form half printed over and a yellow envelope, Tony proceeded to write with his pencil by the light of the now friendly bull's-eye. After a very few moments of writing, he realized that he could never say all he wanted to say on that beggarly sheet of printed paper, with room for nothing but weights and measures. Then a brilliant idea struck him. He asked Mr. Darvel to allow him to speak with Archie alone for a minute.

"Your word of honour, Tony?" was all Mr. Darvel had said; and "Yes" was all Tony replied.

Then the two boys withdrew to their straw, and Tony made the bold proposal that Archie should take his place.

"You are poor and hungry," he said, "and I can't help you except by leaving the tins, and they won't last long. It's a splendid chance!"

"But you don't know Captain Fleming," objected Archie. "He would lash me within an inch of my life when he found me out."

"But," said Tony, after a minute's reflection had brought him a kindly if not very wise idea, "why not pretend to be me? Ned'll stand by you; and when the captain thinks you're a friend of Mr. Campadder's, the owner, he'll not hurt you till you get to the first port; and if he gets nasty there, you can run away. It's easier to get grub in a foreign place than here."

Had the proposal been made at an earlier stage that evening, Archie would not have ventured. But it is wonderful what a couple of tinfuls can do for a boy's courage. Archie agreed to take the chance. Tony thereupon relieved himself from writing at any length, contenting himself with impressing upon Archie the true state of the Sultan affair, and urging him to tell that to Ned the first thing. Then he explained exactly the arrangements for meeting Wallace, and for making the first appearance on deck. While he was speaking he opened his bag, and dropped among the straw the suit of which he had been so proud that morning. But when one is being generous anyway, it is not well to stick at trifles, even if they involve a delicate change of garments in a public shed.

Mr. Darvel and Tony took R36 with them, and it is probable that they gave him a hint. Anyhow he did not return to 37CA that night—at least not till Archie had done with it.

Archie never liked to speak of his first days aboard

the *Arica*. He was not in very good health even for shore, and the presence of sea-sickness and the absence of the tin-opener had driven him nearly crazy. He had not felt hungry in the least till he discovered that the tin-opener was missing. Then he became ravenous, and battered the one tin with the other, and both with pieces of coal, till he became a little delirious, and got into a state that ended with the collapse we have seen.

Ned's satisfaction at the news about Sultan was almost enough to make up for the disappointment of losing the real Tony. He made up his mind to pass on to the new one as much as he possibly could of the old affection.

CHAPTER V.

A TALL YARN.

THINGS soon settled down to a steady order on board the *Arica*. Ned could not have believed, without personal experience, that life on shipboard could be so dull and commonplace. The monotonous sound of the bells, that marked time and regulated the watches, had at first seemed delightful; he thought he would never tire of those charming two bells and four bells and eight bells. The romance did not survive a week. The force of example was too much for Ned, and he growled as loudly as his mates when he had to turn out for duty.

Tony, on the other hand, was quite content with things as they were. Anything was better than dossing on the Glasgow wharves. But Ned felt the disillusionment keenly. He did his best to learn seamanship, and certainly made much more progress than he had done with any of his subjects at Merliston. But it was not quite what he had expected. There were no storms; they hardly ever hailed a passing vessel. It was wet and dull and even cold weather.

Talking to Wallace one night when they were on duty together (Wallace, Treevers, and Ned had been picked for the port watch under Mr. Griffins; while Tony had fallen to the second mate's watch, along with Martin and Scatlan), Ned complained of the monotony.

"If it's variety you want, my boy, you'll not have long to wait. But if you take my advice, you'll be in no hurry. Variety at sea is a little bit wearing. How'd you like three days and nights without turning in at all?"

"Oh, I wouldn't really mind," was Ned's cheery reply. "It's not the turning in that troubles me, it's the turning out."

"You just wait, an' give me your views on the home voyage," replied Wallace, with a grin.

He said no more, which disappointed Ned, who had expected a yarn. To tell the truth, yarns formed an essential part of Ned's idea of life at sea, and here they were on their eighth day out still perfectly yarnless.

When Ned hinted his disappointment, Wallace referred him to Martin, who, when appealed to next day, declared that yarns were not much in his line.

"If you want yarns, you must go to the fo'c'sle."

"But we're not allowed to go to the fo'c'sle, you know," objected Ned.

"No," replied Martin good-naturedly; "but if you're really desperate for a yarn, I might bring a bit of the fo'c'sle to you."

"Have you any really good yarn-spinners forward?" asked Ned eagerly.

"You've seen Old Hookey?"

"Rather."

"Well, Old Hookey is a champion yarn-spinner; different from the rest, too, for he's a literary yarn-spinner—reads ever so many books, and works them all up into his yarns."

Ned was not so enthusiastic on this score as Martin had expected, the fact being that Ned wanted yarns of real life, not book yarns; he'd had plenty of *them*.

"By the way, Mr. Martin, what's the use of Old Hookey on board? He can't do much with his left hand, and the hook isn't much use instead of the right."

"You'd better ask the old man; he's the only

one that knows why the hardest captain afloat burdens his ship with a one-armed man, and gives him extras too."

"How did Old Hookey lose his hand?"

"You'd better ask Old Hookey—he knows best; and that would be a yarn."

Next night Mr. Martin kept his promise, and brought Old Hookey into the deck-house. It was evidently against the rules, for extraordinary precautions were taken, and the old sailor looked enormously pleased. Mr. Martin's rum was of a very satisfactory quality; but it soon became clear that the deeper source of the old man's joy was to be found in the artistic gratification of the appreciated story-teller.

"So you young gents are wantin' a yarn from Old Hookey, hey?"

"Yes, Hookey," replied Martin, as he produced a treasured silver mug of tiny dimensions, but of exquisite design. Inside of it was placed a small glass tumbler that really held only an ordinary wine-glassful. Martin filled this up to the ornamental border, three sixteenths of an inch from the rim, and said, "Campadder, here, thinks sea life is dull, and wants a little excitement."

"Yes, Mr. Hookey," added Ned eagerly; "I want to know how you lost your hand."

The sailor quietly laid down the glass that he had been raising to his lips, and hit the table a bang with the hook at the end of his right arm. Ned did not know that this bang stood for an oath, since Martin had not yet told him that one condition of admission to the deck-house was that there was to be no swearing.

"But I can thump wi' my hook," the old man had stipulated, and the point had been conceded.

Though unable to give a literal translation of this vicious thump, Ned had no difficulty in perceiving that its general sense was dissatisfaction. He thought the old man objected to attention being called to his deformity. He apologized at once.

"'Tain't that," growled the yarn-spinner. "I ain't ashamed o' my hook; but I'm" (here a tremendous whack with the hook on the table) "if I'll stand bein' *mistered*. I'm Hookey, if ye like—Old Hookey, if ye like it better—but there's to be no *mistering* me."

This remark was concluded with a swig that brought the rum-line down to the level of the silver case.

"Well, Hookey, if you won't tell us about your hand, what is it to be?"

"What would you like?" The question was directed point-blank at Ned.

"Oh, something about an island," said Ned; adding, with a blush of which he was terribly ashamed, "maybe with a treasure in it—that is, if you know one."

"*If* I know one! w'y, wot d'ye take me for? As if I didn' know more 'bout treasure-islan's nor any man afloat." Here he looked pathetically round his audience, and sighed, "More's the pity!"

"If I came across a real treasure-island," exclaimed Wallace emphatically, "I would never dip my hands in a tar bucket again!"

"Maybe ye wouldn' 'ave a 'and to dip," retorted Hookey dryly. "Treasure-islan's is dang'rous."

"Never mind him, Hookey; fire away!" cried Martin; and Hookey fired away.

"We was boun' for Frisco, w'en we picked 'im up in a open boat. We was maybe six hunner miles west o' Cape Mendocino, an' it was me as sighted 'im, an' maybe that was w'y 'e took to me. Though maybe I wasn' a lad to be sneezed at in them ole times; a strappin' fellow I was.

"W'en we'd got 'im aboar', we thought 'e was dyin' o' ole age; fur 'is 'air was 's w'ite 's the ole man's Sunday collar, an' 'e 'adn' a tooth in 'is 'ead.

"But it wasn' ole age—'e was on'y two-an'-thirty—it was ill-usage an' foul play. He'd done 'is bes' to get better—'e wanted uncommon to get better—but 'e was too late a beginnin', an' 'e couldn' do't. An' w'en the ole man tole 'im straight 'at 'e 'ad 'is sailin' orders fur kingdom come, 'e looked dazed like aw'ile, an' then 'e asked fur me.

"But 'e didn' want anybody else but me, not 'e. So 'e waits till there was nobody beside 'is bunk but me, an' everybody 'ad lef' us out o' respeck fur 'is dyin' feelin's, an' then 'e sez to me,—

"''Ow'd ye like to 'ave more money'n ye know'd wot to do wi'?'

"'Try me,' sez I, humourin' 'is fancy like, fur I thought 'e was off 'is 'ead.

"'Ye'd 'ave to fight for't,' 'e sez nex', 'an' 'ard too. The brutes ain't no cowards,' 'e sez.

"'Not them,' sez I, kindly like. An' then 'e roun's on me, an' asks wot the—kettle o' fish—I know'd about 'em.

"Then 'e began to talk quite square, an' I was blowed if I could know wot to make o' 'im. I listen'd an' agreed to everythin', jus' to please a dyin' mate, till 'e ups an' w'ispers into my ear,—

"'20° 15' S. an' 121° 37' W., an' don' forget it. Write it down.'

"I wrote it down, an' then 'e tells me that was w'ere I'd fin' a treasure-islan', w'ere 'e'd been bad treated by a lot o' pirits 'at 'ad taken 'is ship an' lots more. Then I began to think 'at maybe 'e was talkin' sense, an' I thought I'd try to corner 'im a bit; so I sez,—

"'But 'ow am I goin' to get to 20° 15' S. and 121° 37' W.? There ain't no packets goin' that way.'

"'Ye'd need a ship o' your own, o' course,' sez 'e. 'An' a tidy crew o' fellows like yersel',' sez 'e, 'if ye want to get the better o' them pigs.'

"*Pigs* wasn' the word, but it'll do. Bein' a dyin' man, I didn' tell 'im wot an ass 'e was makin' o' 'imsel' talkin' o' gettin' ships in that way. But then 'e ups an' yanks out a dagger. I starts back in 'orror; fur though I was a terrible fellow fur fightin' in them days, I didn' care to fight a dyin' man. But 'e on'y wanted to make me swear on the cross o' the heft o't. Bein' a dyin' man, I swore all 'e wanted me to, laughin' in my sleeve all the time, but lookin' awful solemn, so's not to 'urt 'im, bein' a dyin' man.

"But w'en I was done a-swearin' to avenge 'im on a lot o' pirits 'oo 'ad tortured 'im, 'e tells me to feel in 'is shirt near 'is 'cart, an' I'd get somethin' to bust up the pirits wi'.

"I puts in my 'and, an' brings out a dirty little shammy-leather bag; an' 's soon's 'e saw I 'ad it 'e stops bein' a dyin' man, fur 'e was dead.

"W'en I'd time to look into 'is bag, I foun' three stones, biggish stones—one o' them red, one o' them w'ite, an' one o' them blue, jus' like the song. But I'd sense in them old days" (here Martin and Wallace sighed ostentatiously; but Hookey paid no attention to the elaborate insult), "an' I didn' do anythin' or say anythin' till I'd got ashore at Frisco. An' as soon's I'd landed I was makin' my way to the English Consul's, w'en I spies a British man-o'-war in the bay, an' I sez to myself, sez I, 'Well, ole Hookey'—though I wasn' ole then, an' not Hookey neither—' if you're wise, you'll board that frigate, an' ask a off'ser w'ether you've got three glass beads or a fortin.'

"There was bother wi' a younker o' a midshipman; but w'en I'd tole 'im the truth o' wot I wanted, 'e reported to 'is superiors, an' I was sent to the stateroom, an' a off'ser looked a good deal at my stones, an' a good deal more at me, an' then said they was genuine, an' wuth more'n 'e knew. The doctor offered to go wi' me an' see't I wasn' swindled. There's nobody like off'sers, if ye on'y get at 'em.

"I disremember 'ow much I got fur the stones, but I know I got enough to buy a fine square-rigged ship called the *Sleepin' Beauty*, an' fit 'er up fur the kin' o' job I wanted. She was maybe four hunner tun, an' I 'ad no en' o' trouble gettin' up a crew fur 'er. Ye see I 'ad to 'ave goodish men, or they'd 'ave jined the pirits an' 'elped to cut my throat, an' decent sailors ain't too plentiful at Frisco.

"But I did manage to scrape together forty as fine-lookin' young fellows as mysel'. But I 'ad more trouble gettin' mates. Ye see I know'd 'ow to go about gettin' men; but I'd never got a mate afore, an' I know'd nothin' 'bout their articles. An' yet I 'ad to get mates; fur though I was A.B., I didn' know 'bout takin' the sun, an' makin' courses, an' things o' that sort.

"W'en I asks a man called Bolton, 'e says,—

"'Wot you want's not a mate but a cap'n.'

"'Maybe you're right,' sez I; 'an' I'm willin' to ship you as master so long's I sail as owner, an' am master w'en we're ashore.'

"As 'e'd a master's ticket, 'e agreed quite pleasant;

an' 'e got a right good pair o' mates to work wi' 'im, an' a good run we 'ad till we was near the place. An' then I tole my cap'n wot we was really up to.

"'Ye don' mean you've been a foolin' me?' sez 'e, lookin' mighty fierce.

"'No,' sez I. 'A man doesn' gen'rally throw away thousan's o' poun's like that.'

"'You're right,' sez he. 'I've seen the colour o' your money, an' I like it; an' as long's you like to throw't away, 'tain't none o' my business.'

"'Right y' are,' sez I; 'an' wot we've got to do now is to get to 20° 15′ S. an' 121° 37′ W. as soon's possible.'

"Nex' day we was jus' about the place, an' could see nothin',' w'en the mast'ead look-out sings out, 'Lan' ho!'

"'W'ere away?' I shouts, fur I could see nothin' still.

"'Right a'ead,' 'e shouts back; an' we kep' shoutin' for a bit, an' we wouldn' believe 'im: so 'e shins down to the deck, an' runs to the w'eel, an' turns it 'ard aport wi' the 'elp o' the men 'oo 'ad the trick.

"Then 'e turns to the cap'n an' 'xplains 'at 'e *'ad* to do't, or we'd a run into th' islan'. An' then at las' we did see a low an' dang'rous reef not more'n three boat's-lengths a'ead. It was green, jus' like the wa'er, an' no wunner we couldn' see't. The look-out see'd it fro' its roun' shape.

"We laid to, an' lowered the long boat. We 'ad twenty men in 'er, an' one o' the mates an' the cap'n. We was all armed to the teeth, an' I takes my place in the stern sheets, an' seizes the tiller. We foun' we couldn' get nearer the beach nor thirty feet, the wa'er was so shallow.

"Leavin' jus' 'alf a dozen men at the oars to keep paddlin' about in case we might need to leave in a 'urry, we gets out an' waded. The green reef was so slipp'ry 'at we could 'ardly keep our feet; an' w'en we got out o' the wa'er, the dry reef was 'ardly any better.

"O' course I was a'ead o' my men, an' all at oncet I fell down on the rock an' tole my men to do the same. For w'en I'd got to the top o' the reef an' could look over to t'other side, I couldn' 'elp droppin', I got such a scare. I 'xpeckit to see the sea on t'other side o' the reef, an' 'stead o' that I sees nothin' but a big 'ole—think o' that—a 'ole in the middle o' the sea, an' I was afeard some o' the men'd topple over.

"But it was wunnerfuller nor that; fur w'en we'd

crawled to the edge an' looked over, we see'd a beautiful islan' down the 'ole, wi' a ring o' wa'er all roun' it.

"But wot took our fancy more was a queer thing, an' we all rubbed our eyes mighty 'ard to see if we could rub out the queer sight. But we couldn'. There was no mistakin' it. We saw before our eyes a fine clinker-built barque lyin' 'igh an' dry on a little plain on our side o' the islan'. It was heelin' over terrible, but it seemed all right.

"We foun' out later 'at this was the pirit ship *Skyrocket*, an' 'at the islan' 'ad been an or'nary islan' till one day the pirits came 'ome, an' couldn' fin' their islan'; an' w'en they was sailin' a good seven an' a 'alf knots a hour they comes bump agin the tother side o' the reef w'ere the wa'er was deep right up to the reef, an' so the *Skyrocket* 'ad jus' given a little bump an' gone clean over into the islan' down there."

"Bravo, Hookey!" cried Wallace, clapping him on the back.

"Ye may say wot ye like, but you couldn' be more surprised nor us w'en we see'd the 'igh an' dry barque. But as we was a-watchin' 'er we see'd all of a sudden a big bird fly right over 'er.

"'Did ye see that bird?' sez I to Bolton. 'I never see'd so big a one now'ere.'

"'Bird be 'anged,' sez 'e; ''tain't no bird. A big frog, more likely. I've 'eard o' tree-frogs an'—look there; ye see 'im leapin' up that tree!'

"'Bird,' sez I. 'Frog,' sez 'e; an' at it we went till 'e sed 'e'd settle't by shootin' one. He was a middlin' good shot, an' soon brought down one o' 'em on the wing. But as we 'ad forgot to bring a glass wi' us, this didn' 'elp us much at fust, though it did make them queer things show us wot they really was. As soon's the shot 'ad been fired, they 'ad all got be'ind the barque; an' I was a-blowin' up Bolton fur fright'nin' the game, w'en bang goes a gun fro' be'ind the barque, and a bullet goes singin' past my ears.

"They was neither birds nor frogs; *they was men.*"

Hookey gave this startling announcement time to produce its effect; then he went on,—

"We drops like shot on our faces out o' sight o' the queer men, an' I outs wi' my 'andkercher—I 'ad a 'andkercher in them days, bein' a owner—an' fixes it on the barril o' my gun, an' hists it. Then I peeps over the edge, an' there sure 'nuf at the mizzen peak was a w'ite flag. Then I tells t'others to keep still an' out o' sight, an' I gets up an' 'ollers, 'Barque a'oy!'

"Then a frog leaps right across the *Skyrocket*, an' gives maybe three more leaps, an' then it was jus' un'er w'ere I was standin'; but, o' course, 'e couldn' get very near because o' the wa'er. Each o' 'is jumps was maybe sixty feet.

"''Oo are you?' he sings out; an' I couldn' answer, I was so astonished.

"'W'ere's your legs?' sez I; fur 'e 'adn' any, an' was sittin' squattin' like a cat on its hunkers, an' restin' on 'is fore paws.

"'Wot's your business?' sez 'e. 'You didn' come 'ere to ask 'bout my legs. 'Ave you a ship there?'

"'Course I 'ave,' sez I, angry like. ''Ow d'ye 'xpeck me to get 'ere wi'out a ship?'

"'I've know'd cases like that,' sez he. 'Throw's a line, an' we'll come aboar'.'

"'Not so fas', my 'earty,' sez I. 'You must tell me fust 'ow ye got 'ere an' 'ow many there are o' ye.'

"Then 'e tells me wot I've tol' you already, 'bout 'ow the *Skyrocket* 'ad gone over the edge w'ile they was lookin' fur an islan'; an' w'en I kep' at 'im 'bout the nummer, 'e sez,—

"'We're sixty-four all tol'. We was sixty-five afore you did for Cut-throat Bill.'

"He shouldn' 'a said that name; it gave me col' shivers, an' put us on our guar'.

"''An' wot about yer legs?' sez I, sympathetic

like, fur I wanted to know 'ow 'e managed 'is 'igh jump.

"'We've bin a-tryin' so long an' so often,' sez he, 'to get out o' this 'ere 'ole 'at more'n 'alf o' us 'a broken our legs. We couldn' git any grip o' that green reef o' yourn, an' a many o' us tumbled, an' we allus broke a leg. An' then t'others got so cocky about their legs 'at we couldn' stan' it, an' so we cut off all their legs so's to be even all roun'. Some on 'em died,' 'e sez, quite callous like, 'but most on 'em came through't all right, an' then we rigged up them springs.'

"An' wi' that 'e showed me a rod o' iron 'at ran from below 'is belt up to 'is collar, w'ere it was fixed in some way, so's w'en 'e let go the catch the iron bar whacked down on the groun' wi' such a thump as sent 'im spinnin' up in th' air.

"'Clever, ain't it?' sez 'e, quite pleased like. ''Twas our doctor 'oo invented it. He lost 'is legs fust week tryin' to rig up a cable up that—potted 'ead!—reef o' yours.'

"'An' wot 'bout that treasure?' sez I.

"Wi' that 'e gives three 'ops i' the air, an' begins a-sayin' things 'at you younkers shouldn' 'ear, fur 'e sees 'is game was up.

"'Are ye goin' to throw me a rope?' sez 'e.

"'Wot's the market vally o' a rope?' sez I.

"'I'll go an' report,' sez 'e, an' wi' 'at 'e 'ops off double quick to 'is mates. By-an'-by 'e 'ops back, an' sez,—

"'We'll give ye a hunner thousan' poun's fur our passage 'ome.'

"'W'ere's 'ome?' sez I.

"'Cuba,' sez 'e.

"'Too little,' sez I; 'a million's the cheapest we can do.'

"'A million be blowed,' sez 'e. Then we quarrelled a bit, an' 'e went back be'ind 'is barque again, an' we was all a-stan'in' lookin' over the reef, w'en the blackguards fired a volley, an' we was all dead but me. I lies flat down among the corpses, an' didn' know wot to do. An' then I felt 'at I mus' 'ave revenge fur my mates; so I 'alloos to the boat, an' made three o' the men come on the reef to examine the corpses. But they was all dead right 'nough; so we rowed back to the *Sleepin' Beauty.*

"We 'adn' 'alf the men the pirits 'ad, an' we couldn' 'ope to take the treasure by force; but we couldn' think o' leavin' our mates dead there wi'out doin' somethin' to make it 'ot fur the pirits. So I 'ad a plan. We sailed roun' to t'other side o' the islan,' w'ere the sea was deep right up to the shore, an' we began bombardin' the reef. It looked silly at fust, but soon wot I 'xpeckit began to 'appen. The reef began to break down, an' w'ere it broke down the wa'er began to run in, an' by-an'-by more wa'er, an' at las' there was a perfec' curren' settin' in, an' we laughed to think o' the blackguards down there waitin' on their death like rats in a 'ole.

"But all at oncet we began to feel oursel's drawn into the 'ole, an' then I saw wot an ass I'd bin. We was bein' drawed in steady, w'en I comes to my senses, an' stops tryin' to run 'er 'ead agin the curren', an' turned 'er 'ead roun', and made fur a bit o' the reef w'ere it wasn' broke. This was the very thing we should 'a done. We 'ad a bad shock, but the *Sleepin' Beauty* 'adn' up anythin' like the same speed as the *Skyrocket;* so we didn' go over, but jus' stuck a-huggin' the reef.

"But jus' w'en we foun' oursel's safe, an' began enjoyin' thinkin' o' the pirits below, I was 'orrified to see a flag comin' up right i' the middle o' the 'ole—an' sich a flag too! It was the Jolly Roger, no less, an' then I saw 'ow it was.

"I 'ad bin a bigger ass than I 'ad thought; fur we didn' on'y get into trouble, but we was getting the pirits out o't. Fur the *Skyrocket* was a-risin' as fast's the wa'er poured in, an' it was 'er mainmast-'ead 'at we saw comin' up flyin' the Jolly Roger.

"An' the trouble was we couldn' get away, fur the indraught glued us to the islan', an' was doin' its bes' to draw us in altogether. Then the pirits 'ad sixty-four men to our twenty-seven. To be sure their men 'ad no legs; but fur boardin' sixty-feet jumpers are more'n a match fur plain two-legged sailors: besides, there was less o' 'em to get a 'it at wi' our cutlasses.

"'Try to catch 'em on the 'op,' sez I to my men; 'an' at close quarters stick to cut nummer seven.'

"W'en the 'ull floated up to the reef level, the jumpers gave a great cheer, but none o' 'em showed above the bul'arks. By this time the indraught had nearly stopped, an' we did our bes' to get off. We 'ad got fairly started, an' was gettin' a little way on, w'en we 'ears a roar o' cannon fro' be'ind, and down topples our foremast.

"They was middlin' good gunners aboar' the *Sky-rocket;* but by-an'-by they was sorry they 'ad done fur the *Sleepin' Beauty*. More'n 'alf our men was dead, an' the carpenter said we'd 'ad more'n was good fur us atween win' an' wa'er i' the way o cannon balls, an' 'at the *Beauty* was a-settlin'. So we outs wi' the long boat, swarms into 'er, an' makes off.

"We 'adn' gone far w'en we sees 'at somethin' 'ad gone wrong wi' the *Skyrocket*. Ye see, she couldn' 'a bin in fust-rate sea-goin' order lyin' i' that plain; an' it's more'n likely the wa'er was a-pourin' in through a dozen leaks. So the pirits thought o' the *Beauty*, an' came's near 'er as they could, an' then it was fun to see 'em a-jumpin' aboar' 'er.

"But, bless ye, 'twarn no use. The *Beauty* was a-founderin' afore our eyes. But she didn' 'ave time to founder in peace; the *Skyrocket* went down stern fust, an' draws the *Beauty* wi' 'er.

"In a minit or two, w'en the curren's weren' too strong, we paddles back to the place. Fur I wanted to get one o' them pirits, to see wot like 'e really was; I was none too sure they really was men after all. An' then maybe I'd a notion to 'ave one o' 'em stuffed fur the museum at 'ome.

"All on 'em but one 'ad gone to Davy Jones straight, but 'e was a-'angin' on to a spar; so we paddles up to 'im, an' I puts out my 'and to pull 'im aboar', w'en somethin' went wrong wi' 'is spring. W'ether 'e did it o' purpose fur spite, or it was some accident like, I dunno, but 'twas no joke fur me, fur the bang

wi' the iron rod knocked my 'and clean off to the bottom o' the South Pacific."

Here Hookey held up the iron hook that terminated his right arm. It was a dramatic touch. But he was not left long to indulge in sentiment; he had to conclude his tale.

"Of course I was revenged fur my 'and. The ruffian was sent spinnin' into th' air, an' came down wi' an awful splash somew'eres, an' never came to the surface again.

"We was picked up three days later by a short-'anded w'aler, an' we 'ad to go a-w'alin' i' the Antarctic w'ether we would or no. They gave me five poun's fur my long-boat, an' that was the en' o' the treasure fur me. But if any o' you younkers wants a real good treasure, remem'er 20° 15′ S. an' 121° 37′ W.; an' don' forget to take a diver wi' you."

Old Hookey leaned back against the starboard bunk and eyed the third mate significantly. The look meant in plain English: "Don't you think a yarn like that runs to another glass?"

Mr. Martin met the mute appeal by raising the rum-line for the third time to the highest level. By way of asserting his right to this third supply, the old sailor looked round at his audience, and sneered,—

"I shouldn' wunner if some o' you younkers thinks ye can spin a better treasure yarn 'n 'at, eh?"

Ned looked guiltily up, for the old man had expressed the very thought that was at that moment passing through the boy's mind. To tell the truth, Ned was a good deal indignant at what he regarded as a bit of burlesque at his expense. Old Hookey saw his advantage, and pressed it.

"Come on, then; let's 'ave your yarn, an' let's see."

"Bully," cried Wallace, patting Ned on the back. "Let the old sea-dog feel that the whelps can yelp as well—"

"But mine isn't a rigmarole like that—mine isn't a yarn; it's true."

"O' course," grunted Old Hookey; "all yarns is true."

"And we don't yet know where the island is," went on Ned apologetically.

"Islan's need to be looked fur, perticlarly treasure-islan's," said Old Hookey consolingly; "I 'ad a good deal o' seekin' afore I got mine."

Martin added his request; and Ned, not altogether unwillingly, yielded to the pressure.

CHAPTER VI.

AN OLD SEA-FIGHT.

"I SUPPOSE you'd call my great, great, great, great, great, great—"

"I say, hold on," interrupted Wallace.

"Great, great, great—"

"Is 'e often took that way?" asked Old Hookey sympathetically.

"Great, great—"

Martin put his hand on Ned's arm.

"Great, great-grandfather a sea-robber?"

"I can't say about that, but I should say he'd been dead some little time," said Martin. "How many 'greats' did you sling in?"

"Twelve—no, thirteen; and his name was Sir Walter."

"Hullo!"—it was Wallace who spoke—"I didn't know we'd nobility aboard. When did your family lose the 'sir'?"

"Under Mary, I think; we were too poor then to keep up the rank."

"An' yet yer great, great, great, and so forth, was a pirit? I'd 'a thought piritin' 'ud 'a paid better'n 'at."

"*Sea-robber*, Old Hookey," corrected Ned sharply. "It's a different thing attacking armed Spanish ships twice your size, and attacking helpless merchantmen."

"So 'tis, my lad; an' I remem'er oncet on th'—"

"Campadder's yarn, Hookey; you've had your spin," ruled Martin.

"Sir Walter's ship was called the *Unicorn*. It was not a very big ship as things go now, but it was often of great use to the king, being a very swift vessel for that time."

"Maybe five knots a 'our wi' a fair win'," interpellated Hookey contemptuously.

"The *Unicorn* belonged to Sir Walter; but the king looked on it as his own when important service was required, which was only as it should be with a loyal subject like Sir Walter. So one day the king sent for him in a great hurry. It was in 1535, and the Pope was very angry with Henry, and was getting angrier every day. Things came to a head in July, when the king executed Sir Thomas More, after executing the Bishop of Rochester the month before, for refusing to acknowledge him as head of the church. Immediately after the bishop's death, the Pope had made up his mind to issue a bull placing the whole of England under interdict; and though Henry thought nothing of the Pope's anger, he remembered what had happened in the reign of John, and did not want to run any risks till his power was better established. So he sent a secret message to Francis the First of France, who was his friend, to make an alliance with him against the Pope. It is likely that Francis would have done this, because he hated the Spaniards, who were on the Pope's side; but Henry wanted to make sure, and promised something to Francis.

"I can't say what this was, for the message has been lost, but it was something very important for the Spaniards to know, and they somehow got some information about the message through their spies—you know the Spanish spies at that time could find out anything. But Cromwell's spies were nearly as good, and they learned that the Spaniards had found out, and that was why Sir Walter was sent for to the palace. It was Cromwell who did most of the talking. I can't speak like those old fellows," said Ned modestly, "but I've heard the story so often that I've got the whole talk off as it was told to me.

"'The *Bel Age* left London twenty-six hours ago. You know her speed. Can the *Unicorn* come up with her before she reaches Calais?'

"'It depends on the wind, my lord. If any vessel can, the *Unicorn* will.'

"Sir Walter was going to send a message to his men to get ready at once; but Cromwell said he needn't, as he had done that at the same time as he had sent for him. Cromwell had a way of taking things for granted.

"'I can trust you with a secret,' said Cromwell. 'The *Bel Age* is bearing a message of the utmost importance to Francis.'

"Sir Walter bowed very stiffly, for he was a little jealous that he had not been trusted with the letter. But Cromwell soon showed him that Sir Richard Larenne had not been trusted very much.

"'He does not know the importance of his message. The letter is in a case, inside of a cask of wine that is being sent along with some other things as a present to the French king.'

"'You distrust Sir Richard, then?' said Sir Walter, who was little pleased to hear of this insult to a brave man though a rival. 'The king has no better sailor than—'

"'That the king knows; but it has become so difficult to send information without those Spanish hounds getting scent of it, that no trick must be left untried to baffle them. Now, if Sir Richard is captured, the letter will remain safe, for a while at least, till the danger is past; while if he knew of his important cargo, he would almost certainly by his actions let the Spaniards see that he had something hidden.'

"Sir Walter only bowed stiffly as before, being but half convinced; he did not yet see what was to be his part in the business. Cromwell soon made this clear; he was evidently very much worried about the affair.

"'I have just learned from my agents that the Spanish court somehow knows about that wine-cask—how they have found it out I cannot understand—and they have sent off one of their best galleons to intercept the *Bel Age* and seize the letter. They send only one ship, so as not to arouse the suspicions of my agents, whom they know to be keen—though slow, horrid slow.'

"'And my work, my lord?' asked Sir Walter, to rouse Cromwell from his reflection.

"'Your work is to overtake the *Bel Age*, and warn Sir Richard of the nature of his cargo; and to give him this letter, which orders him to burn the letter if he is likely to be taken. If you come up in time, you will go with the *Bel Age* as consort. Even the best of their galleons will not relish an attack upon two such ships as the *Unicorn* and the *Bel Age*.'

"Sir Walter smiled grimly, and said it was all right if once he got within hail of the *Bel Age*, but of that he was very doubtful.

"'God grant that you may!' cried Cromwell passionately. 'More depends on your success than you can ever conceive. But perhaps the hounds only know of the letter. They *may* know nothing about the cask, and hunt only for the letter. It is just possible.'

"You see Cromwell was as doubtful as Sir Walter about the possibility of the *Unicorn* coming up with the *Bel Age* in time.

"The *Unicorn* started within two hours after Sir Walter had been summoned. Everything went well with the voyage. The winds all blew in the right direction, and if Sir Walter could only have known that the winds had been as unfavourable for the *Bel Age* as they were now favourable for him, he would have begun to hope much sooner than he actually did. He thought, indeed, that all hope was gone on the third day out, till a sail at last hove in sight. They soon knew from the colour of the sail—for they sometimes coloured their sails in those days—that it was not an English ship. But though they knew that this was a Spanish galleon, they could not make out whether she was still on the outlook for the *Bel Age*, or whether she had already caught the English ship. Sir Walter did not take long to make up his mind about it.

"'They're making straight for Spain," he said to himself. 'They pay no attention to us, and yet they know that we are English, and we might be the *Bel Age*, and we are not half their size. They have captured the king's ship, and are hurrying home with that letter.'

"All this was true, but it was not the whole truth. Sir Walter didn't know that the little *Bel Age* had made a magnificent fight for it, had fought till the last gasp, and had done such serious damage to the Don's planking that the crew were in rather a hurry to reach a friendly port. In fact, if they did not soon get to some friendly haven, they would never get at all.

"Sir Walter didn't know this, and he didn't care. What he wanted was that letter, and he meant to have it. So he got within range, and let her have a couple of shots that did no particular harm. The Don made no reply for fear of starting more of their planks, and this opened Sir Walter's eyes to the true state of affairs. He knew that something was wrong. He crept up quite close, so that the Don's guns couldn't be levelled at him even if they tried, and peppered away at his timbers.

"The musketeers from the Spanish tops kept up a running fire, and a good many of Sir Walter's men were hit. But everything was on his side, and soon the Spanish commander, under a white flag, made a proposal. He would give up the prisoners he had just captured, and a thousand crowns, if the *Unicorn* would be content to let them go.

"Sir Walter cried back that nothing but the royal letter would satisfy him.

"'What letter?' asked the commander.

"Then Sir Walter was in a mess. Perhaps the Spaniards had not known about the cask, and the letter might be safe at the bottom of the sea, along with the gallant *Bel Age*.

"But then it might not. It might be in the cabin

of that big galleon; and if the galleon escaped, the *Unicorn* would have failed in its expedition. The only thing was to make sure by sinking the Spaniard. So the English gunners began anew. In a very little time the Don hung out the white flag again, and this time the commander acknowledged that he had the letter, and would give it up if Sir Walter would sheer off.

"Sir Walter was pleased, and intended to accept the letter; but he did not want to be too eager, so he asked,—

"'And if I don't, what then?'

"'Then,' says the Spaniard, 'I shall shoot the captain of the *Bel Age* and all his men that are left, and blow up my ship.'

"'Show me the prisoners first!' shouted Sir Walter, for he was far too old a bird to be caught with chaff.

"But it was all right. The captain of the *Bel Age*, with his head bandaged and his arm in a sling, and as much as was left of twenty-three of his crew, were shown on parade on the Spaniard's deck.

"From the sound of the pumps, and from the desperate actions of the Spaniards, Sir Walter knew that the case was very bad for the Dons, and he could easily have sunk them. But what he wanted

was the letter, and what he didn't want was to get
Sir Richard and his men killed. So he said that if
the Dons would give up the letter and the wounded
Englishmen, he would sheer off.

"But the Spaniards would not hear of this. So
long as they had the English prisoners on board, they
had hostages; but if they were given up, what was
to hinder the *Unicorn* from sending the big, crippled
ship to the bottom? It was the letter alone, or nothing.

"Sir Walter knew that they had money, since they
had already offered them a thousand crowns; so the
bargain ended in the *Unicorn* sailing off with the
letter *and* the money.

"At first Sir Walter was greatly pleased with
himself. He had very carefully examined the seal
of the letter. He knew the royal seal well, for he
had often carried such letters before, and he had
made very sure that it had not been broken in any
way. But by-and-by he got anxious. He began
to think that they had been too willing to give up
the letter, and they did not haggle enough about
the money. Maybe it wasn't the right letter after
all. The king wrote many letters; at any rate his
seal was fixed to many letters. Sir Walter felt it
would have been much safer to sink the ship. In

fact. he felt strongly tempted to turn back and sink it yet. But he couldn't do that after making terms; yet he was desperately anxious to see the inside of that letter, in order to make sure. He could not stand the thought of being, by any chance, outwitted by those lumbering Spaniards.

"It is bad enough to open any letter even nowadays, but to open a king's letter at that time was the very worst kind of treason. But the more he thought about the chance of being cheated, the greedier he felt to find out whether this was the true letter. He thought that if it *was* a secret letter, he could keep a secret better than anybody else, and he was the king's friend. He was sure the king would think he had done right if the letter turned out all right, and he was sure he would more than pardon him if the letter turned out all wrong. The Don was just disappearing on the southern horizon, when Sir Walter felt he could stand it no longer. He was a man accustomed to act sharply. He dashed into his cabin, and broke the royal seal.

"In a twinkling he was on the deck, yelling out orders in a fury, foaming at the mouth, and waving the open letter in his hand. For the letter was nothing but a sheet of blank paper.

"He was eager to be at the Dons again, and crowded on all sail. It did not take very long to come up with the poor, stumbling ship. This time the Dons fired.

"'They know it's their only chance, the hounds!' roared Sir Walter, as shot after shot fell wide of the mark. 'I'll teach them to play tricks with a Campadder.'"

At any other time the listeners would have chaffed Ned for his swagger as he repeated his ancestor's words, but the story interested them too much at that moment. Like Ned himself, they felt themselves on board the *Unicorn*.

"As soon as they came within eyesight of the Dons, the English saw a man with a bandaged head and a broken arm standing on the deck along with a score of others. In answer to the English fire these prisoners were dropped one by one overboard, and fired upon from the Spanish deck.

"Sir Walter ground his teeth, and raged; but his business was to sink that ship, at whatever cost. He could not hope to get the true letter now, but he would prevent its doing any damage to the king. When Sir Richard's turn came, Sir Walter foamed at the mouth and screamed his orders, and shook his fist at the Dons. All the same, he kept his ship well out of the way of the other; for he knew that, if he came near enough, the Spaniard would blow himself up, in the hope of carrying the *Unicorn* with him.

"The Spanish guns were worked very badly. As a matter of fact, several of them had been injured in the fight with the *Bel Age*, and the crew were now reckless. They gave up all hope, and stopped the pumping, and the ship lurched heavily. Then the English saw a sort of scrimmage on deck which they could not at first understand; but a moment after, the whole ship went up in a flame with a thundering report, and nothing was left but a plank or two and some spars. The Don had kept his word.

"'A liar and a traitor, but no coward,' was what Sir Walter said.

"He kept sailing about the place for a while, to make sure that no one had escaped, and then he began to wonder what he would do next; for he had no instructions what to do in a case like this. He had no desire to go back to the court to report a failure. He half thought of going off for a cruise on his own hook, as he often did, but he felt that this would hardly be fair. He had begun this business, and must make some sort of an end to it. All at once a plan occurred to him. He would go and report the matter to the French, and tell them what he had done, so that they would be on their guard; and then he would hurry home, and perhaps the king would trust him with the new letter. Brest was not very far off. Three days afterwards the *Unicorn* ran into Brest harbour, where Sir Walter was arrested as soon as he landed.

"But here the sham letter came in handy. He flourished it about, and said he had a letter for King Francis. As this letter was expected, the governor of the place thought it might be all right, and sent Sir Walter to Paris.

"When he got there he was brought before the minister, Antoine du Bourg, and told him exactly what had happened.

"'Show me the false letter,' says the minister; and Sir Walter showed it up. Then a bell was rung, and four archers entered.

"'Take this man to the guardhouse till I send for him,' said His Excellency.

"Sir Walter was not kept long in prison. That very night he was sent for, and the minister explained that everything was all right. The blank letter was not a blank letter after all, but the true letter; only it was written in invisible ink, and nobody but Du Bourg knew the stuff to rub on the paper to make the writing come out.

"'An' w'y did the king get into sich a precious wax abou' 't then, if nobody know'd the secre' but the Frenchies?' asked Old Hookey, with jealous suspicion.

"'Don't you see that the only way the Spanish spies could have found out about the letter at all was from the letter sent first to Du Bourg, and in that letter it was told how the other letter was to be sent, and all about the stuff.'

"'Um!' growled Hookey.

"So His Excellency gave Sir Walter a new letter to take back for an answer, and sent a guard with him to Brest, and thanked him for his gallantry and intelligence.

"And when he got home he went to Cromwell; and Cromwell was so pleased he gave him Arnwyke Abbey and its lands, that had just been seized along with a lot more by the king."

The charm of the story was over, so Martin had a chance to be critical.

"First-rate. But you must keep better up in your dates: Cromwell didn't live quite so long ago."

"But he did; he signed the grant of the abbey."

"Maybe he did; but that only shows that your Sir Walter does not go so far back—is not such a great, great, great, great, great—"

"Oh, I see: you're thinking of *Oliver* Cromwell."

"Of course; and who are you thinking of?"

"Cromwell, Earl of Essex, you know—Henry the Eighth's great minister."

"Oh—ah—yes, of course," mumbled Martin; "I had forgot."

As Martin got up and stretched himself as well as the accommodation of the deck-house permitted, Ned flushed a little, for he was only coming to the part that interested himself the most.

"There's more," he suggested modestly.

"Not for to-night, sonny," replied Martin. "Don't you see that Hookey must be off on important business?" Then noticing the disappointment on Ned's face, he added, "It must be continued in our next. I want to hear the rest.—Have you any pressing engagements for to-morrow, Hookey?"

Entering into the spirit of the thing, the old sailor produced a pocket-book of apoplectic tendency, gravely consulted the needles and strings it contained, and announced that to-morrow would suit him quite well, and it was arranged that way.

CHAPTER VII.

THE CAMPADDER TREASURE.

NO time was wasted in preliminaries at the next meeting in the deck-house. Old Hookey's beaker was filled, with the warning that since he was to be an auditor that evening he must not expect a refill. The meeting was thereupon constituted, and Ned went on:—

"Though Sir Walter got Arnwyke, he was not allowed to take possession of it immediately. Cromwell had an important message for him, and it was necessary for the *Unicorn* to sail at once.

"Now all the monks throughout the country were in a frightful state about the way the king was carrying on with the monasteries. All the treasure in the little monasteries had been seized by the new owners, and the monks sent out to beg. This was only in the small monasteries; but the monks knew that the king was likely to do the same thing soon with the big ones, and all the priests and abbots and things like that were busy plotting to save the treasures in the monasteries that the king had not touched yet. What they wanted was to get the treasures hidden. So when they heard that Arnwyke had been given to Sir Walter, and he had been sent abroad, they thought this was a fine chance to get some of their things safely stowed away. For Arnwyke had a lot of first-rate vaults that nobody knew about except the head monks in the country and the prior of Arnwyke. The common monks of Arnwyke didn't know their own vaults.

"So some of the head monks in the big monasteries made it up with our prior to send their jewels and church vessels and money to be hidden in Arnwyke. You see what a good place it was for hiding. The new master was away, and couldn't interfere; there were splendid vaults, and it was near the sea. The monks had made up their minds to send all their treasures to Spain till the bad times should be past, for they were sure that things would be all right for the church if once this terrible king was dead.

"The monks knew exactly how long Sir Walter was to be away—for they had ways of finding out all that they wanted to know—so they went very carefully about their work. Everything went well. Sumpter-mule after sumpter-mule arrived from all parts of the country, mostly by night, and left their precious burdens, which were carefully stored in the secret vaults. The treasures were nearly all gathered together, when a strange thing happened. Every road for miles around was carefully watched by the spies of the monks, in case Cromwell should hear of the treasures, and send his men to take them. A mouse could not have reached those vaults without the prior knowing. But they did not think of the sea. You see that was the way the treasure was *going;* it did not enter the monks' heads that anybody would *come* that way.

"But that was just the way Sir Walter came. He had no business to be there at that time; he should have been somewhere in France on the king's business. But he had got a hint somehow of what was going on in his abbey, and had hired another man to do the king's business, and had come back to look after his own. The king's business was well done by the other man; but Cromwell never forgave Sir Walter. You see he thought all this treasure should have come straight to the king's coffers. But the whole thing was kept very quiet.

"The monks were in despair, but they knew better than complain to Cromwell, and Cromwell knew better than tell the king how he had let such a big treasure slip through his fingers. But all the same, Sir Walter knew that if Cromwell caught him he would contrive to knock the treasure out of him. So the old sea-dog disappeared altogether with his treasure. It was said that the *Unicorn* could hardly carry it all; but nobody had a chance of knowing, for nothing was ever seen of it from the night when Sir Walter sailed away from Arnwyke, leaving half the monks in the country busy excommunicating him. Cromwell's soldiers came to the abbey only a couple of days later, but there was not even a silver candlestick left for them.

"You may think that Cromwell would have taken back the abbey from our family, but he was too cunning for that. He did not give up hope of getting back the treasure wherever Sir Walter had hidden it. If he could catch Sir Walter, he felt sure he would catch the treasure too. So young Sir Walter was allowed to hold the lands, just as if Cromwell was quite friendly, and his spies all the time were waiting till the *Unicorn* should come back.

"But they waited and waited for nearly five years,

and then Cromwell lost his head, and yet Sir Walter did not come back. Nobody knew then where he spent those years, and nobody knows now, but everybody knows that a man like him would not waste his time when Spanish treasure-ships were plentiful.

"King Henry followed Cromwell, and still there was no sign of Sir Walter. The young Sir Walter was taken to London when Gardiner got into power; but he made it plain that he didn't know where the treasure was, and was allowed to go free. He didn't know he was left free only to be the bait to catch Sir Walter himself. Gardiner was sure the old sea-dog would come back sooner or later, and kept up a constant watch through his spies.

"In 1554, Sir Walter thought he might come home to see his son and his grandchildren. I don't know whether he had written to the young Sir Walter or not, but he must have let him know somehow or other that he was coming, for his son expected him. But so did Gardiner, and the only way I can think of his finding out is by seeing some letter; but maybe he had word somewhere from abroad, where Sir Walter was.

"The father and son were arrested in the abbey the very night he arrived, but they fought like tigers.

Old Sir Walter was knocked down and bound; but young Walter managed to get off by one of the roundabout ways through the abbey, and contrived to get on board the *Unicorn*. It was no good, for there were two of the queen's ships waiting for her, and were far too strong for her.

"But young Walter died game. The *Unicorn* did what she had made the Don do—she blew herself up; and that was the end of one of my ancestors.

"When Sir Walter got to the Tower, he was told pretty plainly that he had to disgorge. If he told where the treasure was, he could go free; but if not, there were such things as racks, and thumbscrews, and boots, and other pretty things to help stubborn mouths to tell things.

"At first he tried to make them believe that the treasure had been on board the *Unicorn*, and had gone up in smoke; but they would not take that in. Then he said that if they'd give him a ship and a Protestant crew, he'd bring back a shipload of gold—not the old gold he had taken from the monks, but fine fresh gold that he had found in new lands, that nobody knew of but himself. They laughed at him, and asked him if he thought they were fools. He was kept in prison a good while, and starved, so as to make him weak.

"By-and-by he offered to guide them to his treasure island, and if they'd give him his freedom and a quarter of the treasure, he promised never to come near England again. He wanted to give the quarter to his little grandson Lionel. But they would promise nothing, and kept on starving him more.

"Then they put him on the rack, and did things to him that used to make our hair stand on end when we heard them from old Fenton at home. He used to like to see us shiver, and maybe he laid it on too thick; but it was awful for Sir Walter, at any rate, and he got weaker and weaker. At last he gave up hope, and one day when they were going to put him on the rack again, he said he would give in, and would lead them to the island.

"But they said they didn't want him to lead them; prison was good enough for him till the treasure was found; after that they might talk about letting him go. You see he intended to jump overboard as soon as he was out at sea, and had had enough to eat, so as to be strong enough to do it. But Bishop Gardiner and his cruel men saw through the dodge, and said that he must tell them where the island was, and they would send men for it themselves; and if it was all right, *then* they'd let him off. But he knew them too well to trust them. As soon as the treasure was found, that would be the last of him. So he made up his mind to die like a brave old sea-dog, and tell them nothing. He was determined they should not have his money.

"By-and-by the jailer saw that Sir Walter would soon die, and the chance of the money would be lost altogether; and Gardiner was dreadfully hard up, and must have money. So they tried a new way. They pretended to take pity on him, and were going to give up trying to make him tell where his treasure was; and they shifted him into another room that was hardly a cell at all, and that had light in it. And they gave him more food and better food, so he soon began to be a good deal stronger. And by-and-by they even let some of his friends in to speak to him.

"But they did too much. When Sir Walter saw that they actually left him alone with his friends, he knew that it was only a trap to get him to let out his secret. He knew the Spaniards too well not to have heard of rooms where every word the prisoner said was heard by a monk, sitting somewhere near with a tube at his ear, let in through some hole into the room; so he took care to say nothing of any consequence to any of his friends.

"But he was allowed pen and ink and paper; so by-and-by he thought he would write a letter telling his brother Arthur where to go to look for the treasure. But he knew that if his letter was caught his enemies would get hold of the treasure; so he had to try to write so that nobody but his brother could understand. This was not easy, so he worried a long time over it. At last he thought of making a map of his island, and marking the place of his treasure. Maps weren't very common then, and most people couldn't understand them. Besides, very few men had dared to sail to the far seas where his island was. So he made a map, and the next time Arthur was allowed in to see him he brought out the map, and kept pointing to it all the time that he was speaking about his grandson Lionel, so as to put the listener off the scent.

"Arthur was a sailor too, and very likely he knew what Sir Walter meant by the signs he made; but I don't see very well how you can tell a man where an island is by making signs with your hands all the time you are talking about something else. Anyway,

Arthur did not get the chance of a long explanation, for in the middle of it the guards came in to lead him off. Sir Walter saw by their looks that they suspected something, and made a queer sign just as his brother was led off. He made the sign of the cross three or four times, on his brow, on his breast, and on the right hand side, and on the left, looking earnestly at Arthur all the time. With any other body it mightn't have been thought so strange, but Sir Walter wasn't in the habit of making signs like that.

"But Arthur had not time to consider the matter much. He was led off to another room, where he was searched and the map taken from him. The captain of the guard grinned when he saw the map, and told Arthur that he would have to stay to keep his brother company, in case he should be lonely, while the queen's men were looking up the treasure. And that was the last that was ever heard of either Arthur or Sir Walter. Very likely the bloodthirsty rascals cut off their heads as soon as they had got their secret out of them; at any rate nothing more is known of them.

"The government fitted out an expedition to go for the treasure, but they could find no trace of the island in the place where they thought it should be from the map; and then they began to see that maybe Sir Walter would have been of more use to them if they had left his head on. But it was too late to think of that now; so they thought of looking up all the Campadders who might be supposed to know anything about the island. But the rest of the Campadders had other uses for their heads, and kept carefully out of the way.

"But while they were hunting for Campadders, a change came over affairs in England. Mary died, and under the young Elizabeth it was the Campadders' turn to hunt. I am not sure which of them it was that managed to catch the captain who had the map; but whoever he was, he thought he had only to get the map to make sure of the treasure. He made the same mistake as the government had made, and was not long in finding out his folly. He sold half the abbey lands to fit out a ship, and sailed away full of hope; but after three years' hopeless searching he came home bitterly disappointed, and gave up the pursuit of the island.

"When the next Campadder was old enough to take his turn, more of the abbey lands went; but the island refused to be discovered. If *we* tried to find an island, we would soon know whether it was there or not. But those old-fashioned sailors could not be sure of anything. Their sailing was guesswork, and they could never be sure to a degree of latitude, and longitude was worse."

"Who told you about latitude and longitude?" interrupted Martin.

"We learned something about it at school, but Briggs the coastguardsman told me more, and the rest I read out of the 'Penny Cyclopædia' in the library at home. Besides, it could not be expected that Sir Walter in prison could give the exact latitude and longitude just from memory, without any maps or charts beside him. So this Campadder was not disheartened, and tried again. But he only lost his left arm and more money."

Here Old Hookey looked up with more interest than he had yet shown, and growled,—

"I 'a noticed that. Money and armses gen'rally does go together."

"But that Campadder's son tried again as soon as he was old enough, and so on for generations. At last our family was so poor that none of them could afford to go treasure-hunting; but they all wanted to go, and there was always some of them going abroad pretending to seek their fortune in India or America, but always really to have a hunt for that island."

"Just like somebody we know about, eh?" said Martin slyly.

Ned looked conscious, and went on,—

"The map got worn away bit by bit, till now it is in tatters—nothing but the rags of a map."

"Yer don' 'appen to 'ave it in yer inside jacket pocket now, hey?" commented the knowing Hookey.

"No: I am sorry I can't show it to you, for my uncle is so wild about our treasure-hunting that he has given away the map to an archæological society."

"Wot's that? A archæol—"

"Oh, a society of old fossils who are fond of other old fossils, such as a map more than three hundred years old. But I've got nearly as good: I've got a good photo of the map."

"'Tain't nearly as good—fur a true story, 'at is," criticized Hookey. "'Ow're we to know ye didn' buy yer photergraph at the archy man's shop, an' the map not yours at all?"

"Show it up, Campadder," cried Martin eagerly; "I want to know what part o' the world your island hails from. I've heard knots o' yarns o' treasure-islands, but never one with a chap carrying a chart in his pocket, and never a yarn-spinner who believed in his yarn as I think you believe in yours."

"I don'," objected Hookey. "'Ow did you know wot Sir Wal'er said in 'is prisin, an' wot 'e intended to do w'en 'e got out, I'd like to know?"

There was certainly room for inquiry here, and Ned felt that the old servant Fenton counted for more in the narrative than it would be pleasant to admit. But he was saved the humiliation of a weak defence by Martin clamouring for the map.

A little sheepishly Ned dipped his hand into the depths of his inner pocket and produced his chart— Old Hookey nodding approval—and Wallace and Martin were soon burrowing into it, while Hookey maintained a somewhat contemptuous reserve. He was a treasure-island yarn-spinner himself.

"Why, it's in the doldrums," growled Wallace. "No wonder your ancestors took so long to discover it. There ain't a capful o' wind there nine days out o' ten."

"How do you know it's in the doldrums, Wallace?" objected Martin. "There's no latitude marked—only that stroke through the middle."

"Yes; but it's marked *Linea*, and I remember enough of my rudiments to know that this reads 'line,'

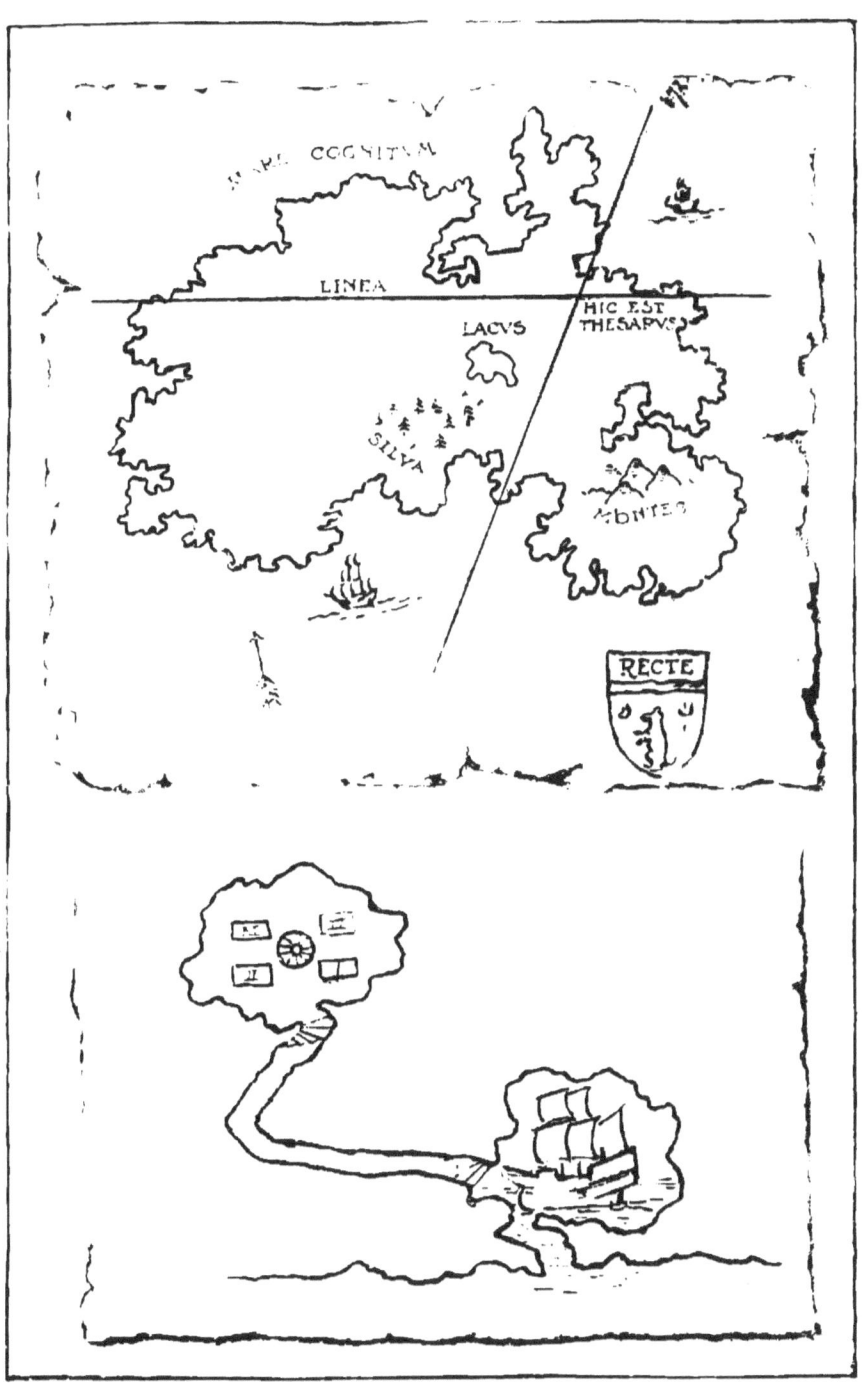

MAP OF TREASURE ISLAND.

and we've had it knocked into us very thoroughly that the *line* is the *equator*, and that the doldrums are handy there."

"That's so," assented Old Hookey graciously.

"But what of the longitude?" said Martin, peering into the dim edges of the photo; "it looks like 72.— Turn up your 'Mercator,' Wallace, and let's see what's to be seen on the line under the seventy-second meridian."

The old atlas with its single remaining board was ruthlessly torn open, and in a few moments Wallace looked up with a quizzical expression.

"Why, your treasure-island's in the heart o' South America!"

"What do you mean?" asked Ned, very quietly, but feeling somehow intensely humiliated.

"Nothing, except that longitude 72°, latitude 0°, lands us in the middle o' a continent. There ain't no islands there, unless maybe your *Unicorn* trotted three thousand miles up the Amazon."

Ned's face fell. This was the first chance he had had of going into the actual question of the island apart from mere story glamour, and it was a little damping, to say the least of it. Martin came to the rescue.

"How do you know it's *west* longitude, Wallace? There's no mark; it might equally well be east. Try the Old World."

"That's better," admitted Wallace, with his finger in the middle of the Indian Ocean. "Seventy-two degrees here gives us a point just to the south of the Laccadives."

"The very spot," grunted Hookey complacently; "them islan's is noted fur their thieves. The very place fur your great, great, great, great—"

"Stow that, Hookey," cried Martin. "I don't think it can be east either, for there was no Suez Canal in those days."

"No, but there was the Cape o' Good Hope," ventured Wallace hopefully; but his firmness died away into the question: "By-the-bye, when did Da Gama round that confounded cape?"

Martin was displeased at having the responsibility thrust upon him; but before he could supply either the information or a rebuke, Ned broke in with his news, fresh from Merliston,—

"1497."

"Well, then, Sir Walter may have hid his treasure in the Indian Ocean, but it seems much more likely that he kept to the west. You needn't be surprised at the 72° landing you in the middle of Brazil. Our instructor at Cardiff, where I was working for my second mate's ticket, told us the old navigators were always going wrong with longitude, and sometimes went as far wrong as fourteen hundred miles. A mistake like that would soon free you from the Brazil forests and land you in the Pacific."

"When did Magellan sail through those straits o' his?" asked Wallace; and this time even Ned could not answer.

"You dry up—you and your eternal questions," growled Martin. "I can't just say what this map means, but it has an honest look about it, and I'd like to look into it.—Will you lend it me, Campadder? I'd like to talk it over with Mr. Griffins, who knows more o' such things than half a score o' rear-admirals."

It was arranged that way. Old Hookey was smuggled to his own end of the ship, and Ned tumbled into his bunk, to think over the new lights, or rather shadows, that had been cast upon his fond dreams.

CHAPTER VIII.

MR. GRIFFINS' OPINION.

IT was two days before Martin had an opportunity of speaking to his superior officer about the map.

At first Mr. Griffins was inclined to pooh-pooh the whole affair; but when he became aware that the map at least was genuine, his interest was rapidly and thoroughly aroused.

"Fifteen hundred and fifty-four he says it is," he muttered, peering into the dim lines of the photograph. "I suppose it's quite possible. But there isn't much here to go upon. What's this printing?"

He got up so as to get the full benefit of the light from the swinging lamp, and read aloud,—

"*Hic thesaurus est.*"

"What's that?" asked Martin, whose education had not included Latin.

"It means 'here lies a treasure'—or maybe it is

only *the treasure*. You didn't tell me the thing was a treasure-island. The lad's been hocusing us."

"I don't think so, sir. It may very likely be all nonsense, and I told him so. But he's as much hocused as we are. He believes in it every word."

"Where did he get it?"

Here Martin told the whole story, as well as he could remember it; and Griffins said nothing, but seemed to listen attentively, and kept his eyes pretty steadily on the map.

"Rather a good story—invented, no doubt, to explain the map. It is probably all tradition, built upon the old map found among the Campadder papers. But all the same it is interesting to try to verify the date. I'd like to hear the boy's story from his own lips."

Griffins evidently thought more of the story than he cared to admit, and Martin was eager to give him all manner of help in his examination. Accordingly he went forward and relieved Ned, who was on duty, telling him that the first officer wished to hear the map story.

It was easier telling the story to this keen, silent man than to the rather critical audience in the deck-house. Mr. Griffins did not interrupt; and when the tale was done, he only said with a smile,—

"So you want to turn treasure-seeker?"

"Yes, sir, in a way; but I want to learn to be a sailor first."

"You'll find it pay better, my lad. Sea-going's a pretty poor business for money-making, but it's miles ahead of treasure-hunting as a steady thing."

"Do *you* think the story is true, sir?"

"I can't just say off-hand what I think," was the slow reply. "I don't know exactly what to think about it. It seems to me to hang together all right, in a way."

"But what about the longitude? Mr. Martin says the mistake could be easily made by an old-fashioned sailor. Maybe they didn't know about longitude and latitude at all then."

"You say this map was made in 1554. Well, then, Mercator must have been about—about, say, forty-two years old, and I should think he had made his great invention by that time. Sir Walter might very well have heard of the new kind of maps."

"Yes; but the line is squinting—not like the lines in Mercator's projection," objected Ned, who remembered how at Merliston he had preferred Mercator's straightforward style of map-drawing to the groggy curves and parallels of the ordinary maps.

"We can't make much of that," answered the officer, drumming on the table with his fingers. "You see those old sailors were not very particular about their lines and their charts. It was mostly learned men on shore who made charts, but *they* were far too particular again. Those old longshore sailors were all land-locked Ptolemaics."

"Yes, sir?" said Ned, very doubtfully, putting into his tone the question he did not dare to put into words. Mr. Griffins kept drumming on the table, and waving the photo backwards and forwards in his hand, evidently worrying over something. Ned at last could stand it no longer, and boldly asked what a Ptolemaic was.

"Oh, a Ptolemaic! ah, I daresay I shouldn't have used that word. It really isn't a word, you know; I just made it up. Eh, well—it does look like it!—what was I saying?—oh yes, about Ptolemy."

Here Mr. Griffins pulled himself together, and noticing the look of wonder on Ned's face, gave his full attention to the explanation.

"You've heard of Ptolemy, of course?"

Now everybody *has* heard of Ptolemy, but not one in a hundred knows more about him than his name.

Ned had heard of him repeatedly, but he did not happen to remember who or what he was. To tell the truth, he was not quite sure whether Ptolemy was the man who fought against Cæsar or the man who was drowned in crossing the Red Sea.

"He was a warrior, wasn't he?" Ned ventured cautiously, thinking that this description would cover both cases.

"Maybe he was—most men had to do a little fighting in those days—but he's best known as an astronomer. He thought the sun went round the earth, and—"

"Oh yes, sir," interrupted Ned eagerly, "and Galileo said it went round all the same."

"You've got your stories mixed up a little," said Griffins, with a smile. "But you're right to bring in Galileo, though he wasn't born when this map was made. He was just the sort of man who wanted to see things for himself, and not believe all that old writers like Ptolemy said. For Ptolemy had made maps in his day—his day was more than seventeen hundred years ago—but his maps did a good deal of harm to sailors; for those longshore sailors kept on making all the mistakes that Ptolemy had made, and wouldn't hear of anything against Ptolemy. They would believe Ptolemy rather than their own senses."

"Is this map full of Ptolemy's mistakes?"

"That's just what I don't know. I don't think it. You see your Sir Walter was a real sailor who sailed, and not a man who sat in his arm-chair at home and spun fine theories with rulers and compasses. He saw with his own eyes, and—it may be a coincidence, but the more I think of it, the more it looks like it. But it would revolutionize the history of nautical discovery; and yet what has that got to do with the truth—if it is the truth?"

The officer had wandered off into something that was interesting himself, and it was not till he had caught the puzzled expression on Ned's face that he pulled himself up, and exclaimed,—

"I say, Campadder, you'll leave that photo with me, won't you? I don't think there is any *treasure* to be got, mark you—I don't want you to make any mistake about that, for it could only land in disappointment—but yet it may turn out to be a treasure in itself, this map, something the British Museum would give a good deal for, and will make you—or me—famous—if I'm right."

Mr. Griffins' voice died away into an undecided

whisper, and Ned felt that now was the time to take himself off.

When he reported the result of this interview to his friends in the deck-house, Tony criticized the officer's conduct in a way that raised quite a new set of ideas in Ned's mind.

"That's the best news you've had yet," commented Tony. "I've noticed that. It's always the same. Whenever you tell a man about a treasure-island, he laughs at you, if he thinks it's not true; but if he thinks it's true, he says it isn't true, *but he doesn't laugh.* He's thinking how to get the treasure for himself. Your Mr. Griffins knows there's a treasure, and he's going to get it; but he's too honest to steal it all, so he's made up his mind to pretend the map is worth a great deal of money, and then buy the map from you, so's to pay you back your share of the treasure."

Tony had learned in a hard school not to trust anybody. Everybody wanted to take advantage of everybody, according to him. Ned, who had as yet learned different lessons, did not agree with him, and tried to show that he was mistaken.

"You just wait," retorted Tony. "The next time you see him he'll talk all about the map, and say nothing about the treasure, and I'll lay ten to one he'll offer to buy the map in the museum at home."

Next day Ned was sent for again, and sure enough all the talk was about the map. What Mr. Griffins wanted was the tale of Sir Walter all over again; but all the questions he put were about the map—not a word about the treasure. After the tale, which Ned had no difficulty in repeating almost in the same words as before, so thoroughly had he learned it from old Fenton, Mr. Griffins gazed at the map intently, and dismissed the boy, telling him he would make up his mind about it soon.

Ned returned to the deck-house; but Mr. Griffins, map in hand, went on deck, and moved over to where Martin was on duty. The day was fine, and everything was going well. Martin, though on duty, was quite free to discuss the map. For some reasons Mr. Griffins would have preferred to talk over the matter with Roylston, the second mate. But though older than Martin, Roylston was not nearly so clever, on the bookish side of seamanship at any rate.

"What do you make of it?" asked Martin, with interest.

"To tell the truth, it puzzles me more than I care to own to Campadder. But tell me, Martin, which island does it recall to you? Answer straight away, without thinking too much, or you won't be able to answer at all."

After a quick glance at his superior to make sure that he was in earnest, and a long stare at the map, which he turned about at all sorts of angles to try to get up a resemblance to something else, he gave it up.

"I can't see any likeness to any place I know. There's a bit at the bottom with three prongs that looks a little like Greece, but that's no good. Greece isn't an island."

"I hate to make wild guesses, Martin, but I fancy I can trace a resemblance to an island you know. But it's so improbable that I'd rather you came to the same conclusion yourself without my saying what it is. Now, what struck you as most peculiar about Campadder's story?"

"Well, it struck me as very peculiar that a man with such an immense treasure should go on sailing; all old sailors, you know, hunger for dry land, and want to be farmers."

"Yes, yes," interrupted Griffins impatiently; "but what struck you as most peculiar when Sir Walter was disturbed by the guard coming into his room?"

"You mean crossing himself?"

"Yes."

"I daresay it was rum enough, now you mention it. Sailors are superstitious enough, but not too religious as a general thing. And, by-the-bye, Sir Walter was a Protestant, wasn't he?"

"Have you ever seen a man crossing himself?"

"I can't say I have," answered Martin, in some surprise; "maybe I have, though—I can't remember. But what's that to do with it?"

"Well, in crossing they don't draw lines; they only indicate points by tapping on the forehead and breast. Do you happen to remember any cross made up of points like that?"

"Do you mean the Southern Cross?" This very doubtfully.

"Yes," said Mr. Griffins, looking very significantly at his junior officer; who, however, made no sign of comprehension.

"If that coat of arms weren't a coat of arms but an island," continued Mr. Griffins, trying a new tack, "which island would it remind you of?"

"Tasmania?"

"Yes." Again the searching look, and this time there was an answering glance of intelligence from Martin.

"You don't mean to say you think it stands for Australia?"

"Well, I don't go the length of definitively saying it *is* Australia, but doesn't it look a little like it?"

"But Australia wasn't discovered till—till—"

"The year 1660," supplied Mr. Griffins.

"But if it wasn't discovered till 1660, how on earth—"

"Don't you see that the whole point lies there? *So far as we know*, Australia was unknown till the Dutch discovered it in 1660, and Cook explored it. But that does not prevent a certain Walter Campadder, who had a good deal of loose time on his hands, from discovering it long before. America was discovered by the Norsemen long before Columbus was born, you know."

"Yes; but if he had discovered this huge island, why didn't he make it known? If *I* had discovered—"

"Don't you see that the story explains all that? Sir Walter had certain reasons for keeping his knowledge to himself."

"But how could he, with a cockle-shell of a boat, cross the Pacific?" asked Martin incredulously, but looking puzzled, all the same.

"Naturally, I've thought over all that. In the first place, what do you think was the tonnage of Columbus's three cockle-shells—his one-decked ship and his two caravels? One hundred and fifty to two hundred tons. Then in the times that Sir Walter was sailing, some of the king's ships are estimated at as much as one thousand tons. Sir Walter's might be five hundred or even six hundred. Is there anything to hinder a vessel of that size sailing from the Thames to Sydney harbour?"

"Well, no; I suppose smaller ships have done it. But they knew the way, and they knew that there *was* an Australia to go to. They have all sorts of appliances too. Those old navigators liked to hug the shore; they were afraid of the open ocean."

"Remember this was nearly half a century after the discovery of America. The Cape of Good Hope had been doubled. Sir Walter does not seem the sort of man to hug the shore; he appears to have been ambitious. My idea is that he rounded the Cape in the usual way, intending to make for India, but that adverse winds drove him out of his course. After the stress of weather had passed, and it was possible for him to steer north again, he may have kept on his southward course through a daring curiosity to know where it would land him. Or he may have made a wild guess at the true position of India, and have literally gone astray into the Eastern Archipelago, and been led on from island to island, until he reached the great Austral continent. Eh?"

"Well, maybe," replied Martin, who had been closely examining the map during this speech; "but it doesn't look really like Australia—except Tasmania."

"And the Gulf of Carpentaria, and Queen's Channel, and Cambridge Gulf. York Peninsula is no doubt too short, and not properly shaped, and Spencer Gulf is ridiculously exaggerated, and Shark Bay much too far inland. But those are the very things you have to expect. If the map were really like Australia as we know it, I should be inclined to suspect its authenticity altogether. As it is, its very defects are its strongest points. Have you ever seen a map of that period?"

"I can't exactly say. I've seen a lot of old maps, but I can't say about their exact dates. But hold on—if it's Australia, what about the 72° meridian?"

"If you look carefully into the map, you'll see it isn't 72°, but 172°, and that's one of the strongest arguments in favour of Australia. I've been looking up some of my books and notes, and find that those old navigators began their longitude somewhere—I can't exactly make out where*—just to the west of Spain, and carried it right round to 360°. In one old map, of just a little later date than this, the longitude ends with the Malay Archipelago, which it puts in under the 180th meridian. The island can't be in the Atlantic, for the three hundreds begin immediately after the point west of Spain. Of course the 172 is a blunder, but for that time the guess at the longitude is exceedingly accurate."

"It may be 172," said Martin, doubtfully eyeing the blurred figures; "but what do you make of *Linea* in that case? No part of Australia reaches the equator."

"No; but this line is not necessarily the equator. It seems to me that it is quite a modern fashion to speak of the equator as 'the line.' As a matter of fact, those old map-drawers always represented the equator and the tropical arcs by *double* lines. The equator is, I am almost certain, always represented by a double line with black and white spaces, just like a scale. Of course, it does not follow that the equator could not be represented by a single line, but it makes

---

* The first meridian was really drawn through the Fortunate Isles, which seem to be the Canary Islands.

it at least probable that this line does not represent the equator."

"Then what *does* it represent?"

"That I can't say just off-hand, but it may have something to do with the treasure story."

"But it would take Sir Walter years to make Australia at the speed he could get up with his old *Unicorn*," objected Martin after a minute.

"It would take him very much longer than even our slowest ships; but the story of the map makes full allowance for that. I questioned Campadder particularly about that, and so far as the story goes, Sir Walter had years to make his voyage in and do his explorations. Then there is that remark about new gold. May it not be just possible that— But no; the treasure is placed far from any of the goldfields."

"Then you really think it is Australia?" asked Martin, staring hard at the photo.

Now Griffins did not like this way of putting it. What he wanted was opposition that he could meet and objections he could overcome; for he was far from being convinced himself, and wanted to gain assurance by argument. He did not like to be put into the witness-box in this way.

"Well, to tell the truth, I think it is. But there is one difficulty that you haven't mentioned, and which is to me the most serious of all. The outline of the map is complete, as you see, and to make even an inaccurate map like this implies far greater care and attention, and deliberate map-drawing intention, than we have any right to assume in an old sea-dog like Sir Walter. Why should a mere adventurer spend his time in exploring a continent 2,400 miles long and 1,800 miles broad?"

"Well," replied Martin, taking his turn at the defence, "as you said just now, he had more time on his hands than he knew what to do with. And then he was ambitious; maybe he thought of setting up as King of Australia."

"Maybe. But what about Tasmania? Does it give no hint? Campadder tells me that the coat of arms is not the Campadder crest, nor is it the least like it. He has no idea what the drawing means."

"Oh," cried Martin eagerly, "is it possible?" Here he laughed, and concluded a little sheepishly, "That queer beast there at the bottom looks like nothing so much as—at any rate, isn't it possible —well, what do you say to it for a *kangaroo?*"

Griffins stared at his companion for a moment, to

see if some petty joke was meant; and after making sure that nothing of the kind was intended, concluded the conversation by saying, as he put the photo into his pocket,—

"As likely as not."

CHAPTER IX.

A COUNCIL OF COLONELS.

A COUPLE of days later, Mr. Griffins again invited Ned to come and have a talk with him.

"How would you like if Columbus was your ancestor?" he began.

"Splendidly. But—what do you mean?"

"Whether would you discover that treasure, or find out that you were descended from Columbus?"

Ned was in a tight place. He felt that it was very greedy to think more of the treasure than of fame, but, all the same, the money seemed so much more substantial. He answered evasively,—

"I don't suppose I'm going to get the choice, so it's hardly worth troubling about."

"I'm sorry for that," replied Griffins, rightly interpreting Ned's answer; "for I think we may manage to show—thanks to this map—that Sir Walter was as great a discoverer as Columbus."

"Yes," said Ned, with big eyes.

"What would you say if I proved to you that Sir Walter discovered Australia more than a hundred years before the Dutch knew anything about it?"

"Why, what do you know about it? What have you discovered? Does the map say that?"

Then Griffins put Ned through much the same catechism as he had put Martin through—with this difference, that Ned, seeing fewer difficulties, was more easily convinced.

But with conviction came a disquieting consideration.

"But if it's Australia, what about the treasure? If it was a little island, we would know where to look for it; but in a place like Australia we would not know where to dig—the mark may cover hundreds of miles."

"Oh, the treasure," muttered Griffins indifferently. "That's a very different matter. If you ask my opinion, it is that you should give up for ever all thought of that will-o'-the-wisp."

"But if the treasure isn't true, the island isn't true either, and it can't be Australia."

Griffins was annoyed at this turn of the talk, but had no very good argument to offer.

"By the way, Campadder," he asked, by way of turning Ned's flank, "did Sir Walter in the story ever *say* he had a treasure *anywhere*? or have you not quietly assumed that, because a treasure was lost, Sir Walter must have found it?"

For a moment Ned was put out. He could not remember any explicit statement by any one that Sir Walter had actually had the treasure with him at the time when he came home. Perhaps he had lost it; maybe it had really gone up with the *Unicorn*. But then a happy thought struck him. He simply pointed to the map, at the words *Hic thesaurus est*.

"Right you are," said Griffins thoughtfully. "But maybe *thesaurus* merely means a place for making a fortune. Queensland is a very rich country, you know, and he may have marked a spot there as a good place to settle in away from all the persecution of England—just like the Pilgrim Fathers in America."

Even Ned knew enough history to think this a very unfortunate comparison—this old sea-dog of an ancestor of his and those stern old Puritan exiles. But he had sense enough to make no commentary, and returned to the deck-house trying to make as much out of the glory of an exploring ancestor as out of the hope of a brilliant heritage in the way of treasure. If he had no longer a golden dream before him, he had gained an even more glorious past than he had ever dreamed of.

"Didn't I tell you?" was Tony's triumphant comment when Ned reported Mr. Griffins' discovery. "You see the treasure's nothing, the map's everything; you'll get lots of folks to tell you that."

"But think of the glory of being descended from the man who discovered Australia," put in Ned.

"Glory be blowed. Give me treasure for my money. What's the good of having had a great-grandfather at the discovering of Australia?"

"You underestimate your case," said Martin: "you mean a great, great, great, great, great—help me out, Campadder—grandfather."

"And besides," struck in Wallace, who was nominally on duty, but who joined in the conversation, "isn't there some right to the man that first plants his flag in a new country? isn't it his, or something like that?"

"To be sure; I'd forgotten," cried Martin, suddenly getting up and dropping melodramatically on one knee.—"Hail, King Campadder!"

"That's all you know about kings," commented Tony. "Don't you know that kings have only their front names? You mean King Edward the First of Australia."

After the bowing and scraping of the three courtiers had lost some of its novelty, the talk became quite serious, and those lads, as ignorant of the first principles of law as they were of Chinese, gravely debated on the rights and privileges of the discoverers of unknown lands.

When the discussion had nearly burned itself out, Tony returned to the charge, saying emphatically,—

"You may talk, and talk, and talk about laws and rights; *I*'m going to keep an eye on that treasure. If the map's not Australia, we must find out what it is; and if it is Australia, we must look for the treasure just about the south-west end of York Peninsula."

"Do you intend to plough up half of Queensland?" asked Martin sarcastically.

"I'll tell you when we get there," was the reply; "we don't even know yet whether the treasure is buried in the ground."

"Of course not; I forgot. Maybe it's up a tree; or no, I'll tell you what—you'll find it's been left for safety in charge of tame kangaroos. You'll see them hopping about there by the hundred, each of them carrying a bit of treasure in her pouch. But how'll they know we're the true heirs? we've no papers—just this photo of the island."

"We'll manage when we get there," was the dogged reply.

"But we're not going to Queensland, my lad; we won't go further north than Sydney, and maybe no further than Melbourne, and that's fourteen hundred or fifteen hundred miles from the treasure kangaroos."

Tony made no reply, but his look was so full of significance that Martin felt it to be his duty to mention it to Mr. Griffins, who made a mental note that if Tony and Ned turned out to be sailors that were really worth retaining, it would be well to keep a sharp lookout over them while in Australian ports; while if they turned out to be useless, it might pay to let Tony in particular have all the opportunities he wished.

The arrival at Rio was an anxious moment for both Tony and Ned. They were terribly afraid that some unpleasant message might be there waiting for them. The message, however, was of the pleasantest. It contained an order to Captain Fleming to enter the new apprentice on the ship's books as Archie Campbell. This looked very suspicious; but as the premium had been paid to the owners, it was none of the captain's business. The thing was done. But Archie was called into the captain's room, and was straitly commanded to retain his name of Tony Wedgeworth so long as he sailed in the *Arica*.

"You're Campbell on our books, and nobody knows what you are in reality; but you began with us as Wedgeworth, and Wedgeworth you'll remain: and if you breathe a word of this to anybody, you'll repent it."

The captain was determined that no chance should be given for tales about his one stowaway.

Mrs. Wedgeworth had obviously yielded to the real Tony's prayers, and had paid the premium; for Uncle Roland was not the man to remit even thirty pounds.

By the time the *Arica* approached Melbourne, Mr. Griffins had quite made up his mind that both the lads were worth keeping. They had made great progress in their work, knew their duties and did them, and were altogether turning out a credit to the ship. To be sure there had been no room for heroism. The passage had been intensely dull, so far as weather went. They had had the usual dirty weather at the usual places, the usual calms where calms are general, but nothing at all out of the common.

Yet, since it was their first voyage, the boys did

not find life at all dull on board the *Arica*. The changes in climate, the new supply of stars, the actual working of cordage and spars that they had heard so much of in books, all gave an interest to everyday life that made weariness impossible.

When the coast of Victoria might be expected at any moment, the interest of the two boys became intense. They expected something wonderful at the antipodes, and they kept telling each other that they would be certain to be disappointed; yet they went on expecting, all the same. They did not quite "expect to see the treasure round the corner," as Martin had suggested, but they could not deny that they expected something.

It was Tony who brought the matter to a practical issue by reminding Ned that Mr. Griffins had retained the map. It was only after a very great deal of persuasion that Ned screwed his courage up to the point of approaching the first officer on the subject; but when he had stammered out his wish, he was astonished at the answer,—

"On the whole now, Campadder, don't you think I'd better keep the map till we're well out of Australia? You know I'm responsible to your uncle for your safe appearance on our return."

If Mr. Griffins had ever had any doubts about Ned's real intentions, they disappeared now. Every feature in the boy's face pleaded guilty as he quietly returned to the deck-house to report progress to Tony. The latter looked very solemn over the matter, so Ned tried to cheer him up by reminding him that if they could not get off to look up their treasure, neither could the first officer. Queensland was just as impossible for him as for them.

The *Arica* was to be delayed at Melbourne for three weeks, or probably a month; yet no sooner had she been comfortably settled in her berth in the harbour, and the official formalities attended to, than Mr. Griffins went ashore—a very unusual thing for a first officer, who is expected to be shipkeeper in port— to talk to some shipping agents that he knew. In their office he looked up the city directory, and then addressed a letter that he had written on board some days before. The inside of that letter told a little— not too much—about Ned's map, and on the outside he now wrote:—

COL. ROTHERHYTH, R.E., F.R.G S., F.Z.S., F.R.S.E.,
 Corresponding Member of the Royal Geographical Society,
  The Marsupial Club,
   MELBOURNE.

This was all he had time to do on shore that day, for he had much to do on board; but next afternoon he took the two boys ashore, and showed them some of the sights. At first they were inclined to be indignant at being led about like schoolboys; but they soon got over that, and enjoyed their afternoon.

When they reached the *Arica* again, they found a large square envelope, addressed, in big quill-written characters, to "Mr. Richard Griffins, First Officer, *Arica*." On the back were a good deal of embossed printing and a slab of red sealing-wax.

Hastily tearing open the note, Mr. Griffins rapidly ran through it, and looked up with pleasure. It was better than he had expected—no less than an invitation to dinner. He had not hoped for more than a lunch.

"This is an invitation to dine with Colonel Rotherhyth, on Thursday, Campadder, at the Marsupial Club. Do you accept?"

"Why does he ask me?" inquired Ned, looking guiltily at Tony, who ostentatiously looked the other way.

"Because the map's yours, I suppose; and he wants to know all about it. Of course we'll go. We do not need to dress like landsmen; he says we're just to come in our blue jackets."

When Mr. Griffins went away, Tony turned round to his companion and asked what he thought of that for cheek.

"There he goes, giving away your treasure just as if it was his own. I shouldn't wonder if they put your map in the papers. I wouldn't put it past them; and when we do get up to Queensland, we'll see nothing but the hole. The half of Australia will be up there digging before we get clear of this ship."

"But the colonel's a gentleman, and wouldn't dream of stealing our treasure; and if Mr. Griffins wants it for himself, why does he tell the colonel?"

"I don't know," was the gloomy reply, "but I know he's something in his eye. Maybe the colonel's to do the digging while we're going round to Sydney."

"Rubbish! who ever heard of a colonel digging?"

The fact was that Ned was rather impressed by the grand envelope and the thought of dining with a colonel. When he actually reached the Marsupial, his gratification was greatly modified at finding Colonel Rotherhyth in ordinary evening dress. He had expected full regimentals. The disappointment was a little relieved when he found that the three other gentlemen who were guests along with himself were two of them colonels and one of them a commander.

They were only visitors in Melbourne, like Ned himself, but that made no difference in their grandeur. All four were big, gruff-voiced men, all grey, but none of them bald. I have been told that it is one of the secret rules of the service that no colonel shall become bald.

During the dinner, Colonel Rotherhyth naturally played the chief part; but as soon as the map story came on, the commander, as an expert in naval affairs, took the lead. All four seemed to know a great deal about geography.

Ned quite enjoyed telling his tale. He knew it so well now that he could calculate exactly the effect each bit of it would have on an audience. At least he thought he could, and maybe as regards an ordinary audience he was right. But those old warriors baffled him. They listened and nodded and smoked, and asked questions all in the wrong places. When the tale was told, the commander asked if the map was the only remnant of Sir Walter.

"No sword, or casket, or book, or pen, or anything left?" he queried.

"No, sir; the *Unicorn* was blown up, and that was the end of her. Sir Walter was never heard of after this map was seized."

"That's bad," commented the commander; "it gives a mythical look to the whole story. If we could have shown even a letter, or a book with his name on it, or a relic of any kind. Why, Sir Walter's hat would have comforted many a superstitious geographer."

Then they began to discuss the map, and Ned found that he was of no more consequence. All their attention was taken up with a certain major that those four old gentlemen seemed to think a great deal of.

Ned consoled himself by paying a great deal of attention to the fruit that the old gentlemen were shamefully neglecting. The boy could not help wondering why full colonels should think so much of what a mere major had to say; but he by-and-by found out that this new man was not even a major, but only one whose name was Major. But plain Mr. Major had found out and proved, it seemed, that Australia had been discovered by the Portuguese long before Torres sailed through his own straits in 1606, or the Dutch ship *Duyfhen* had landed in that same year at Cape York.

Mr. Griffins had heard only of the Spaniard and the Dutchmen, and was a good deal disappointed when he found that somebody had been before him in proving that Australia was known in the early fifteen hundreds. But, after all, as he pointed out to the geographers, even if the Portuguese had discovered Australia, they had not made such a good job of it as Sir Walter had done. They had left no trace worth speaking of; at any rate, they had left no map.

"The fact is," proclaimed the commander pompously, "that the existence of a great Austral continent was suspected for centuries before Australia was actually discovered, and the suspicion was no doubt often pushed to the extent of asserting the existence of that continent. I should not be surprised if Wytfliet, for example, wrote his description entirely from hearsay. This discovery, if authentic, is a much more important thing, and shows a complete knowledge of the country."

"Including Tasmania," added Colonel Rotherhyth, "which was supposed to be unknown up to 1642. It's a very remarkable discovery."

Then the old gentlemen came to what was the real business in hand, and started to discuss what was to be done about this valuable discovery. About some things they were unanimous. First, they agreed that the map should be reproduced by some process, and that each of those present should get a copy. This was very cordially arranged. Secondly, a copy should be sent to the headquarters of the Royal Geographical Society in London, along with a full report of the peculiar circumstances under which the discovery had been made. It was here that difference of opinion arose. It soon became clear that Colonel Rotherhyth wanted to write this report, and send off the communication to the society.

"You see, I'm corresponding member, so I suppose I must write to headquarters," he said easily, as if he were making a martyr of himself.

Nobody said anything; but the commander pulled his moustache, and looked around surprised that no one had already suggested that, as a specialist in naval matters, *he* should be asked to write the report. As no one took the hint, the silence became oppressive, till at length Mr. Griffins came to the rescue with an offhand suggestion.

"Probably I'd better do it myself, since I was the first to suggest the idea that the map represented Australia."

Again the oppressive silence, during which the two nameless colonels looked as if they were hunting for some plausible excuse for putting in a claim on their own account. The colonels, the commander, and the mate all knew that whichever name went to London with the map and the report, would be handed down to posterity in the "Transactions" of the society, and that seemed to them to mean immortality. Mr. Griffins now regretted having consulted those geographers. It is true they had given him confidence by examining and accepting his theory, but now they were trying to rob him of the glory of it. He thought bitterly that America should by rights have been called Columbia. He did not consider that if Australia as a name were to be given up, it should be changed into Campadderia rather than into the barbarous Griffinsia.

"Probably a joint report would be the best," suggested Colonel Rotherhyth as a compromise. "I shall write it, and the commander will sign it, and you too, sir."

The concluding words were addressed to Mr. Griffins, who certainly did not seem at all mollified by the attention. It was from the dissatisfied face of his officer that Ned gathered courage to interrupt,—

"But what about my treasure?"

Had the four old gentlemen been the treasure-stealers Tony would have made them out to be, they could not have been more thunderstruck by this speech. The treasure had not for a moment entered into their calculations. All their interest had been in the geography, and they were at a loss to answer this question. Mr. Griffins alone remained undisturbed; in fact he looked rather pleased than otherwise.

Gathering courage from the abashed faces of the four strangers and the relieved look on his officer's face, Ned ventured to make the demand that Tony had insisted upon his making.

"I'd—I'd rather not have the map published till I've searched for the treasure."

"Well, if you expect to find a treasure because an ancestor put a mark on a map three and a half centuries ago, you are of a sanguine disposition," growled old Rotherhyth. "But certainly the map is yours to do what you like with.—However, I do not suppose you will object to my writing a report on your discovery."

The last sentence was addressed to Griffins, who found himself in a fix. He thought at first of getting Ned to refuse, but he felt it would be too petty to hide behind a boy; so he took the bull by the horns, and said quietly,—

"I should prefer that in the meantime no report be sent."

"Why on earth did you consult us then?" asked the colonel angrily.

"I consulted *you* personally on account of your well-known knowledge of geography and your great interest in cartography. I did not consult the others."

The colonel saw that he had gone too far; the commander was a little ashamed of his recent selfishness too: so the slight flutter was soon over; and bearing the map, the two Aricas parted very cordially from the geographers.

"They'll report, all the same," growled Griffins—"in a general way, of course. But they know now where the map—the real map—is exhibited; and all those London folks have to do is to run down to Sardon-super-Mare and examine the thing at first hand. I say, Campadder, you won't object to my writing a full report of my theory and sending it home?"

Since Ned saw that the thing was now public, he preferred that a friend should get whatever glory was to be got. So it was arranged that Griffins was to write, and at once, so as to forestall the colonels.

Mr. Griffins did not turn in that night at all, but a bulky blue letter, which he posted with his own hands at the central post-office, seemed to comfort him for his loss of sleep.

CHAPTER X.

NEW LIGHT ON THE SUBJECT.

AFTER sending away his report on the discovery, Mr. Griffins made up his mind to write a monograph on the subject and have it published when he got home.

With this in view, he spent a great deal of time in studying the map and writing about it. What he found hardest to explain was the word *linea*. The position of the equator was well known to navigators at the time the map was made, and though several of the Portuguese and other navigators in their charts had placed Australia too far north, none of them had gone so far astray as to place nearly half of it north of the equator.

Mr. Griffins was almost certain that *linea* did not mean the equator. He had found that in all the old maps he could lay his hands on the equator was called, not *Linea*, but *Æquinoctialis circulus*. But he had no satisfactory explanation to offer of what *linea* really did mean. Day after day he puzzled over this word, twisting it about into all manner of peculiar shades of meaning. Sometimes he had to deliberately leave *linea* and turn to something else, to prevent himself from losing his head altogether.

One day, worn out with *linea*, he had turned listlessly to the shield underneath. Suddenly lifting his eyes from the shield back to the *linea*, his memory carried the *recte* up to the *linea*, and unconsciously the one ran into the other. The English, not the Latin version of the word, came into his mind, and he aimlessly muttered,—

"Rectilinear, rectilinear."

Half a minute he kept muttering; then he was down upon the map with a swoop, questioning it with his magnifying-glass. Had those words *recte* and *linea* any connection with each other? This was important, but still more important was the question whether this compound word had any connection with the many little straight lines that varied the general waviness of the outline. He had not noticed before that there were such bits of *right lines* among the generally very undulating contour. What did they mean?

These were the questions that he feverishly put to

himself, but no answer was handy. It now seemed incredible to him that he had not sooner observed the connection between the two words, for he now felt convinced that there was a connection. He boggled for a long time over the point where the two lines crossed—the *linea* and the 172° meridian—but could make nothing of that. That evening and the next passed without any solution.

On the third evening Ned was called into the cabin, where Mr. Griffins was sitting alone. On the table in front of him lay the everlasting map, on which he had evidently been drawing. Ned had never seen Mr. Griffins look so unhappy. Obviously it cost the officer a great deal to restrain himself as he said,—

"Well, Campadder, I'm inclined to think Sir Walter did not discover Australia after all."

"No, sir?"

"No. At any rate, I think I have found another explanation of this whole map. I really believe now that it was originally a treasure map, though I fear the treasure is long ago gone."

"I don't understand, sir."

"Of course not; let me explain. Take your own map" (Mr. Griffins had had the map photographed in Melbourne, and had given Ned a fresh copy), "and show me one or two straight lines in the contour."

Ned did as he was directed, and was astonished to find how many of them there were.

"Now, suppose you produce all those lines with a pencil—here's a straight-edge—and see what happens."

Ned began, but drew the lines only a little bit out.

"Further out," said Mr. Griffins; "I want you to see where they point to."

Ned did as he was told, and to his astonishment found that he had drawn a cross on the map, as any reader may see for himself, if he cares to produce all the little right lines in the contour.

"This puts a new complexion on the Southern Cross, eh?"

"Yes, sir," said Ned vaguely; "but what does it all mean?"

"I cannot undertake to say what it means, but I have very little doubt what it does not mean, and that is Australia. Confound that report I sent off! How I wish I had let the colonel do it! How I shall be laughed at!"

"But Sir Walter could not want to play a practical joke on his brother," said Ned; "besides, he wanted

Arthur to know it was a cross. Maybe there's an island right enough somewhere, and this cross is to help to lead to the treasure. Eh! do you notice that the two lines cross each other just at the very corner of the arm?"

"Do they?" cried Griffins, recovering his interest for a moment; then falling back into his usual listlessness, he muttered, "Let them meet; what do I care? I've had enough of the miserable island. Take it away."

Ned's news had quite a different effect in the deck-house. Tony was charmed. This discovery had all the elements that belong to the story of a hidden treasure. The theory that the island was Australia had damped the treasure theory completely. But this cross revived all manner of possibilities.

"All we have to do," cried Tony enthusiastically, "is to find that island and draw a cross on it, and there, at the left-hand lower corner of the middle crossing, is the treasure waiting for us. It's almost certain to be a very small island, and so it will be easy to find the money."

"Yes; it's likely to be a very small island," criticized Martin; "so it'll be easier to discover it, seeing you have only the world to search for it. There's only five hundred and eighty-two islands on the west of Scotland; what's to hinder us beginning there? We've only to draw a cross on each of them, and dig at the left-hand lower corner of the middle crossing, and there you are. If there you aren't, why, then, hey for the next island!"

"But why did he put in the cross at all?" objected Ned, "when the two long lines give the point exactly already. The cross tells us nothing new."

"I daresay you're right," said Martin, knitting his brows; "and that puts a new face on the whole thing. The cross must have been a sign of something else, for Sir Walter expected his brother to understand him. Was there any cross in the abbey that Sir Walter might have hid a key to the puzzle in, or maybe a true map?"

"I don't think it. You see the abbey was burned down, at least most of it was, by Cromwell's soldiers, and there's now scarcely any of it left, nothing but the masonry marks on the ground where we used to play when—"

"Well?"

The colour was coming and going in Ned's face. He breathed with difficulty, so lively was the excitement under which he was labouring.

He was in no hurry to answer. A gleam of memory had flashed an idea into his mind. He felt that he had got at the bottom of the mystery.

"To tell the truth, Mr. Martin, I have an idea, but I've been so often mistaken that I want time to think it over before I say any more."

"Oh, very well," growled Martin ungraciously; "you know your own business best, I suppose. Maybe you'll take my advice next time I offer it."

Ned made no reply, but waited his chance of talking with Tony alone.

"I know now where the treasure is, Tony, and I want to see what we should do. I didn't tell Martin till we had talked it over, you're so suspicious. I was afraid to speak in case you'd find fault."

"Where is it, and how do you know?"

"It's at home in the abbey, buried at the left corner of the nave and transept, looking towards the altar."

"How in the world do you make that out? And what about the island?"

"You see the cross here? Well, what's the use of the cross? It doesn't show anything new about the spot, because the two lines, the *linea* and 172°, show that spot where they meet. But the cross must show something, and that something is the shape of the chapel where the treasure is hidden. We used to play about the ruins of the old chapel. There is scarcely one stone left upon another. But we know the shape of the old chapel quite well; every corner of the cross was a goal in some of our games."

"But is that all you have to go upon? What about the island?"

"The island was only put in to blind the queen's men. The important thing—what Sir Walter wanted to tell his brother—was the cross."

"That's like enough," assented Tony doubtfully.

"But then there's that arrow that we couldn't understand. If it shows the points of the compass, which direction would you say it pointed in?"

"North, of course."

"And if that is north," said Ned, putting his finger on the map, "in what direction does the aisle run?"

"East and west."

"Well, doesn't that about settle it?"

"What has east and west got to do with the church?"

"Don't you know that a chapel always goes east and west?" asked Ned, in amazement at his friend's ignorance.

"No, they don't—not always, anyway—in Scotland. Do they always go east and west in England?"

"Always," replied Ned, with a show of confidence he did not feel; "at all events, all the old chapels run east and west, just like this one."

"It looks all right," assented Tony thoughtfully; "but I thought the abbey had been searched up and down before it was burnt."

"Yes; and that is the very reason why Sir Walter came back there to hide his treasure. Nobody would think of looking for it among the ruins. Besides, the secret passages and store-rooms all opened off the chapter-house, and went westward. Very likely they were searched over and over again, and that would keep the queen's men from ever thinking of Sir Walter's hiding anything under their very noses."

"D'ye know, Ned, I'm beginning to think you're right."

"Should I tell Mr. Griffins this time?"

"Oh yes. It's different when the treasure's at home, among civilized folk. You can't do what you like in England; there's law there—*I* know that. It was desert islands I was afraid of. Oh yes, you should tell him."

Encouraged by this gracious permission, Ned went

aft, and asked Mr. Griffins if he might speak to him. On the permission being wearily given, Ned proceeded to lay his new explanation before his superior officer, who, in spite of himself, got gradually interested, and ended by clapping Ned on the shoulder, with the words,—

"You've got it this time, and the treasure's yours without a doubt. It's rough on me about Australia; but those geographical fellows were as much off the rails as I was, and after all they didn't find out their mistake at all, like me. So they can't laugh so very much."

"Wedgeworth was talking about that, and he says your plan would be to say no more about it for a good while, and they'd all prove that it was Australia, and then you could come down on them and score off *them*."

"That lean little rascal has more worldly wisdom in his little finger than you and I have in our united heads, Campadder. He's right. I'll just let them fight it out among themselves. There's sure to be two parties, and monographs and counter-monographs. So I'll keep quiet till both sides have committed themselves; then I'll come in, like the god from the machine, to put matters straight."

"Besides," added Ned, "it would keep the secret of the treasure safe."

"There speaks Wedgeworth, I wager; that idea never came from your own head. So *that's* why he took so much interest in my affair."

"Well, he said that if a hint got out that the old abbey had treasure, every stone of it would be upturned within a week, and not the shadow of treasure would be left for us poor Aricas."

"By-the-bye," remarked Griffins thoughtfully, "I hope you'll have no difficulty in making good your claim to the treasure, if you do happen to find it. Did it legally belong to Sir Walter or to the state?"

Here was a new, a very unexpected difficulty. Up till now it had not arisen, as Ned never thought of the law of the matter at all, and Mr. Griffins had not up till now considered the treasure question seriously. The two talked it over, and came to the conclusion that there could not in fairness be any doubt as to Sir Walter's having a right to the treasure. The Campadders' right to this prize was exactly the same as that of the Russells and Cavendishes and other families, now great, that had taken their place among the great ones of the country because they had been enriched by the spoils of the monasteries.

"And if the worst comes to the worst," concluded Griffins, "you can claim the treasure because it was found on your land."

Worse and worse. This reminded Ned that the abbey was no longer the property of his family. A letter from Uncle Roland had told him that Arnwyke had been sold to an old pottery manufacturer called Brownjohn. Uncle Roland thought he had done a very fine thing, for he had got an excellent price for the property, and he thought that by the sale he had made it impossible for any more Campadders to lose their heads treasure-hunting.

"Maybe he'd think differently now," complained Ned, as he finished telling Mr. Griffins about this new trouble.

"We must make the best of it," commented the officer. "I do not suppose that the new proprietor will object to our search for the treasure; and if it is once found, I do not expect that you will have any bother in establishing your claim."

"But if we tell him what we want—he's a close-fisted old curmudgeon, I am told—he'd at once search for the treasure himself; and if he found it, who'd it belong to then?"

"Really I don't know. You see, if he found it

himself in his own grounds, I'm afraid the law would be hard to convince that it didn't belong to him."

Ned's face fell.

"But it won't come to that, my lad. Besides, by the way, it isn't a case for common-sense, but for the lawyers, and we never know how they'll look at a thing."

But as they would not be in England for at least other five months, they felt that there was no special call for hurry in making up their plans. A treasure that had waited for nearly four hundred years would not complain about an extra month or two.

Accordingly, Ned went back to the deck-house a much less happy boy than he had come, and left Mr. Griffins a much happier man than he had found him.

When Martin had been conciliated, and induced to listen to the explanation of the true meaning of the map, and the new difficulties that had arisen in treasure-hunting, he added a new difficulty of his own.

"It seems to me that the treasure's neither yours nor Brownjohn's, but the Queen's. It's treasure-trove, and all treasure-trove belongs to the Queen."

"But," objected Ned, "if I lose a sixpence, and Tony finds it, must I send the sixpence to the Queen?"

"That's different, for there you know exactly who lost it; but," he added, with that dogmatism that almost everybody who knows no law assumes when speaking of legal matters, "anything found anywhere that doesn't belong to anybody belongs to the Queen, and goes to the crown."

"I wish we hadn't told him," muttered Tony; "he does nothing but find faults."

But Tony was mistaken. Martin did not confine himself to pointing out difficulties; he had a plan.

"Your best plan is to say nothing about it to anybody, but land quietly near the abbey, search for the treasure through the night, and go off early in the morning again, till you get the treasure. As soon as you've found it, lump it off bit by bit, and nobody'll be the wiser, and the Queen won't be any the poorer. She has lots without that, and she would never get it anyway. It would never get her length; it would be stopped by some old, bald-headed man sitting on an office-stool in some government office in London."

It was agreed that this was the best way. For a future occasion was left the consideration of how to obtain a boat sufficiently large to carry off all the treasure they expected to discover.

When Mr. Griffins was consulted on this new

difficulty of treasure-trove, he had no information to give, but he promised to ask the first time he was ashore at any port. But all his inquiries met with no satisfactory answer. Treasure-seeking is a little out of the ordinary run of business, even in an office mainly given up to shipping matters; so it is not surprising that the legal agents at the various ports declined to give an authoritative opinion on such a delicate and unpractical problem. They had all a general impression that the money went to the crown, but they would not commit themselves to any hard-and-fast rule. It was not till the *Arica* had got home, and had put into Cardiff, that a really satisfactory lawyer could be consulted.

Mr. Griffins took Ned to the office of a certain firm —Kimball, Clerson, and Dibble—which had a good reputation there. It was Mr. Dibble who received them. It is remarkable that lawyers like to run in threes, and it is always the third one on the list that you see when you call—maybe because the third man, like the third time, is lucky.

After the manner of lawyers, Mr. Dibble wanted to ask questions rather than answer them.

"Is the treasure you have found within the United Kingdom?"

"We haven't found any treasure," explained Mr. Griffins. "We consult you in order to find how the law stands on the subject."

"Then the treasure you expect to find, is it within the United Kingdom? You see my answer depends upon yours."

"Well, the law that we want to know about applies to the United Kingdom," was Mr. Griffins' cautious reply.

"You'd be better to tell me your real case." (This is what lawyers always tell you.) "But if you do not care to do that, I must make my answer very general, perhaps too general to be of any use. It is not the law that is difficult; it is the application of the law to special cases."

Then leaning back in his chair, Mr. Dibble proceeded to give a short lecture.

"To begin with, *treasure-trove* means money or valuables of any kind hidden in the earth or any secret place. If ownership can be established, it ceases to be treasure-trove, and reverts to the heirs-at-law. Genuine treasure-trove belongs absolutely to the crown."

Ned's face fell. The lawyer was now sure that he was on the right tack, and went on,—

"Any one who discovers such treasure must, by law, at once report it to the authorities. Not to do so is a CAPITAL OFFENCE."

As the lawyer gazed keenly at Ned, the boy felt suddenly uncomfortable about the throat. He had great difficulty in keeping down his hand, which seemed determined to go up to see that his neck was all right. Mr. Griffins took a different line.

"I do not remember," said he quietly, "of ever hearing of a man being hanged for hiding such a discovery."

"No," was the calm reply; "such cases are necessarily rare. Besides, they now usually commute the sentence to penal servitude."

"But that is barbarous," replied Mr. Griffins: "the man who discovers a treasure should be rewarded, not punished."

"I may say," went on Mr. Dibble, to soften his somewhat severe deliverances, "that it has become customary of late years for the crown authorities to reward the finders of such treasures, if duly reported."

"What percentage, now, might the reward be of the value of the treasure-trove?" asked Mr. Griffins, anxious to get as full information as possible, for Ned's benefit.

"Well, it has become usual, in the case of small sums at any rate, to reward the finder to the extent of the value of the thing found."

"Do you mean the market value?"

"There has been no decision on that point; and, further, it must be kept clearly in view that such a reward is purely voluntary on the part of the authorities. The treasure belongs absolutely to the crown."

"Now, suppose I find a treasure in the field of another man: who gets the reward?"

"The reward being meant for the finder, it follows that it does not matter where it is found, whether in one's own field or in another's."

"Now, suppose there is a tradition in a certain family that a certain ancestor left a chest of money hidden in a field, say four hundred years ago, and a member of that family digs it up now: to whom would it belong?"

"To supposititious cases I can give only supposititious replies. If the tradition were clear that the money really belonged to the ancestor, it would undoubtedly fall to the finder, if the finder happened to be the heir-at-law of the ancestor in question."

"In such a case would it be necessary to report the discovery to the authorities?"

"Undoubtedly."

"Now, suppose that in the meantime the estate had fallen out of the hands of the family of the original proprietor: would that make any difference in the case?"

"It would certainly complicate matters, and increase the necessity for clear proof of the original ownership of the treasure and the relationship on which the claim was based. But, pardon me, a family that claims to trace its members through four hundred years generally has a family lawyer. Don't you think he'd be the best man to consult?"

Mr. Griffins saw that Mr. Dibble was annoyed at not being trusted with a full statement of the case, yet he did not feel himself at liberty to divulge any more at this stage; so he quietly said that probably the family lawyer would be the proper person to fall back on, and, after paying the not very large fee demanded, came away with Ned.

"My advice to you is to run up to London at once, and consult your uncle, telling him all about the affair, and maybe he'll make terms with Brownjohn. If he won't, it will be time enough then to think of trying Martin's rough-and-ready plan."

CHAPTER XI.

UNCLE ROLAND RELENTS.

THE following evening Ned made his appearance in Uncle Roland's drawing-room, where he felt altogether out of his element. He was much bigger now than he had been when he had last been there some two years before. He was bigger all over, but his hands seemed to have got bigger in proportion, as ship apprentices' hands have a way of doing, from continually dealing with ropes and mops. It was a great trouble to him to find some place to put his hands out of the way, they were so big and red. His aunt and cousins, to be sure, were particularly kind, especially the girls; but Ned didn't want to talk to girls, and felt inclined to quarrel with the boys. What he wanted was to see Uncle Roland alone. This wish was soon gratified. It was then that the trouble began.

It was easy talking to Tony about the treasure.

Wallace and Martin believed in it, and even the critical Mr. Griffins had at least an interest in the map, as a map. But this ruddy-faced, prosperous merchant, by his very look, seemed to make treasure-hunting a thing to blush for.

"Well, my lad, I *am* glad to see you again, looking so well and strong and hearty. I may say that the reports on your conduct and progress are excellent—from all parties—excellent! Nothing like the sea for blowing away superstitious cobwebs. No more word of treasure-islands now, hey?"

This was a bad beginning. Ned felt that after this he could not begin to urge his uncle to buy back Arnwyke in order to save the treasure. He only looked sheepishly up at his uncle, who interpreted the guilty look as a confession of the foolishness of former childish ideas about the island.

"Come, don't be ashamed of it, Ned, my boy. We've all got our little weaknesses, and you're very fortunate in getting over yours so early. Stick to plain, straightforward, solid hard work, and your boyish romancing will do you no harm. But you wanted to see me alone—on business, hey? A holiday, isn't it, to run down to Sardon and see all your old haunts?"

The temptation was too much for the boy. He

could not bring himself to talk to this terribly matter-of-fact uncle about treasure. He fell in with the suggestion, and begged for a month's holiday. He could at least spy out the land, and make ready. At any rate, anything was better than introducing islands at that moment.

"You'll find everything wonderfully changed down there. That old skinflint has enclosed the whole grounds by a ten-foot wall; it looks liker a prison with its grounds than a respectable house. No more visitors at Arnwyke now. The little inn is going to change hands soon. Mrs. Peterson cannot make ends meet, it is said. Why, you'd think our famous treasure was in the abbey itself, to see the way the old curmudgeon goes on."

Ned's face grew long. He knew Mrs. Peterson, and liked her, but her misfortune could hardly account for the look of keen anguish that passed over his face. It seemed to him that everything was working against his ever getting that treasure. It was not so much that he feared this new wall would keep him from getting at the treasure. A ten-foot wall is not so much as a circumstance to a sailor. The trouble was that all those precautions looked as if old Brownjohn had some idea of where the treasure lay hid.

"I wonder if he suspects anything?"

The words had slipped out before he knew that they had been uttered aloud. He saw, too late, by his uncle's face that their meaning had at least been guessed.

"What could he suspect?" This very dryly, from Uncle Roland.

"I just wondered if he suspected that the treasure was hid in the abbey itself."

"Yes; and from your hang-dog look I should imagine that you had some such absurd idea yourself."

There was so much contempt thrown into the words that in self-defence Ned launched out into an oration in which he proved his position, and supported it by the evidence of Mr. Griffins and the others who believed in it.

Uncle Roland listened with wonderful patience to this hurried explanation. Ned could not make it out. He did not know that his uncle and Mr. Brownjohn had quarrelled upon almost every question that had arisen since the transfer of the property. Anything that promised to give the new owner of Arnwyke an advantage was very unpleasant for Uncle Roland.

"I wish I'd known this before I sold the abbey. A treasure-island with an absurd map is mere March madness; an old abbey with an unexplored corner is quite a different affair."

Uncle Roland did not care to mention that the real cause of his uneasiness was the remembrance of certain conditions that Mr. Brownjohn had contrived to insert into the transfer deed without exciting any attention. One of those conditions had expressly included in the sale everything under as well as upon the surface. Immediately after the sale the meaning of this condition had become clear, for Mr. Brownjohn had at once begun to work a certain kind of clay, of the value of which only an expert like himself could be aware. This had greatly angered Uncle Roland, who had all a business man's dislike to being outwitted in a bargain. He pretended that he was enraged at the mess the new man was making of the estate by grubbing up all the fine lawns and parks, but his anger was really due to the feeling of having been bested by a mere pottery man.

But now this new suspicion cast a still more lurid light on the possibilities of that awkward clause. It was bad enough to think that this fellow was making a good thing out of a chance that ought to have come to the Campadders, but to face the possibility of this pottery man sweeping in a treasure that had been waiting in the family for four hundred years was more than human nature could stand. So long as it was a matter of common-sense, no one could be calmer or wiser than Uncle Roland; but this was no longer a matter of common-sense—he wanted to be even with this disagreeable old potter.

"What do you propose to do, Ned?" he asked, in a tone that very agreeably surprised the boy.

"We intended, Tony and I, if you gave us permission, to reside in Brendown for a while, staying there all day and coming over every night to search the abbey—if we could get a boat."

The last words were put in rather wistfully, and not unskilfully. But they produced no reply. Uncle Roland was busy thinking, so Ned had to go on.

"But now that you think the treasure *may* really be there, wouldn't it be easier just to buy back the abbey? then we could search for it comfortably."

"Don't be a jackass, Ned."

This was a little rough on Ned. How was he to know that Arnwyke had turned out to be worth more than four times what Brownjohn had paid for it? Uncle Roland knew, hence his sharp answer.

"Then," ventured Ned again, "should we try it the way we thought of?"

"But even if you found it, he could claim it under the *sub terra* agreement."

"I don't think he would, sir. We consulted a lawyer, and he said it would belong to the crown."

"You consulted a lawyer, you young rogue! You young folks *are* going ahead. But, after all, I don't know that I can do any better than follow your example. I think I'll look round and see Mr. Sarginiss to-morrow forenoon, and I think I might do worse than take you with me."

Next day it took a great deal of questioning and counter-questioning before Mr. Sarginiss caught all the points in the case. Then he said that, after all, he would like to take advice before giving a definite opinion.

"But all this while we're losing time, and there's more people know our secret," objected Ned.

"As to time, I shall give my opinion this afternoon; and as to more people knowing, you forget that lawyers are like dead men—they tell no tales."

"Remember," said Uncle Roland, "we don't want a written opinion; you can tell us all that is necessary by word of mouth. I want no records of this interview."

After all, Mr. Sarginiss did not consult anybody in particular. He did talk in a general way with a fellow-lawyer with whom he happened to have other business; but that was a mere accident. What he really wanted time for was to consult his books. For lawyers cannot be expected to carry all the law about everything in their heads at once. Mr. Sarginiss had never had a treasure case before. But he did what every good lawyer would have done—he read up all about it that afternoon; and when Ned and his uncle called, they found him choke-full of information about treasures.

Leaning back in his chair, with his back to the light and his finger-tips resting against each other, he laid down the law as he understood it.

"Several ways of raising the point may be suggested. First, Mr. Brownjohn may discover the treasure. In that case he claims it or its equivalent from the crown as treasure-trove. You can then put in your claim as Sir Walter's heirs-at-law, and so far as I know your case, that claim would be sustained. In that case it ceases to be treasure-trove, and becomes your property, liable to the usual legacy duty."

"Oh, in that case no more need be said," interrupted Uncle Roland. "It does not matter who discovers it, since I can make good my claim, or Ned's claim, which is the same thing."

"Pardon me, it is not quite so simple," continued Mr. Sarginiss politely. "So soon as you have made good your claim, Mr. Brownjohn will bring in his *sub terra* clause; and since the treasure really belonged to you at the time that the property was transferred, the deed of transfer, being duly executed, naturally conveys the treasure to him. There might be a slight chance of fighting on the rights of a minor, since Master Edward here was no party to the transaction. But the chances of success in that direction are not encouraging, seeing that you bought the estate legally from his father."

"Then, after all, nothing does remain to be said," complained Uncle Roland. "It looks as if Mr. Brownjohn were playing a 'heads-I-win, tails-you-lose' game with us. If I can't prove my claim, he seizes it as treasure-trove; if I can, he snaps it up under the *sub terra* clause. I don't have even Hobson's choice."

"Well, it isn't quite so bad as that either," replied Mr. Sarginiss soothingly. "There *is* a way. Suppose some one, *not* Mr. Brownjohn, finds the treasure—say Master Edward here—and you do *not* make clear your claim to it as heir-at-law, then it is treasure-trove, and it falls, or its equivalent falls, to the said Edward Campadder."

Mr. Sarginiss beamed upon Uncle Roland, who did not for a moment see the point, but then objected.

"But Edward *is* the heir-at-law. There is no shadow of doubt about that. The line is as direct and clear as the Queen's."

"Precisely. But while it would be very easy for you to prove your legal claim, it would be exceedingly difficult for another, say Brownjohn, to do it for you. If no claim is made from your side, the burden of proof lies with Brownjohn, and I think"—here the lawyer looked knowingly over Ned's head at the uncle—"that we know a place or two in the tree where only we could keep matters straight. In short, if you make no claim, that treasure falls to whoever finds it."

"Thank you, Mr. Sarginiss; I think I am now past all need of further help. Your share in this business will not be forgotten, believe me, if anything comes of it. Good-day."

"You've got to discover that treasure, Ned, if there is one. I think your plan is the best possible; only you'll need more help than your friend Tony can give. Wallace is now free; do you think he would come?"

"Rather," cried Ned, dropping into an unusual familiarity with his uncle.

"Martin will be useful too, but too young to manage an affair like this. I wonder if we could spare Griffins too, for a day or so; there's Wilkinson we could send in his place. That's it.—Hey, cabby, 49 Linthouse Wharf."

* * * * *

Captain Fleming nearly lost his wits when he received his owners' telegram telling him to send on his first mate and his third and two apprentices; though, of course, Wallace was leaving at any rate, and was only waiting for Ned's news before quitting the *Arica* for ever.

"Why doesn't he send for the crew too, and the lumpers, and the cook, and have done with it, and send me word to discharge the cargo myself?"

Then glaring around the deck, he clamoured,—

"Hullo, you Martin, you're to pack up at once and report yourself to the owners in London."

"Yes, sir," replied Martin, looking the surprise it was not convenient to express otherwise, and turning over in his mind all the evil deeds that his conscience might have mislaid.

"Bundle up; it says *immediately*," cried the indignant captain, referring to the telegram, and frowning because Martin had given him no cause to break out. Without a word the third mate made for the deck-house. Before he reached it he heard the further order,—

"Get Wallace and Wedgeworth to pack up too; they're wanted along with you."

This fresh information supplied Martin with a clue. He began to see that Ned's business was at the bottom of this. Evidently he had been successful in convincing the old gentleman at last. So the three were quite merry as they packed all that they thought necessary for the train journey.

Mr. Griffins happened to be ashore on ship's business, and did not return for a couple of hours, by which time the captain had cooled down.

He would have cooled down in any case in talking to Mr. Griffins, for he never succeeded in bluster before his first officer. But it was easier to be quiet now, for a second telegram had arrived, saying that Wilkinson was on his way to take Griffins' place for a couple of days.

The four travelled very comfortably up to London, where Ned met them and took them to his uncle's office. There Mr. Griffins had a long talk with his owner, while the youngsters amused themselves as best they could in a very dismal sort of waiting-room.

When Mr. Griffins appeared again, he told them they were to go at once to Brendown; not by Sardon, the usual way, in case the arrival of four sailor lads should attract attention, but by the long way round by the Grey Chine. This meant a nine miles' drive, which was certainly not an unpleasant beginning.

"Of course I'm not going with you," he concluded, to their great disappointment; "you are to be under Martin's orders, and I've no doubt he'll give a good account of himself."

Then the first officer went off to Houlston and Bamber's to arrange about the hire of a long boat, to be sent to Brendown for the expedition.

"You're to play the part of a sort of tourist for the time, till your ship is ready to sail. You're to be fond of fishing, for fishing, you know, is much better carried on by night than by day, and you want to avoid suspicion."

"Do you mean an open boat with a lugsail?" asked Ned, with disappointment in his voice.

"Yes; did you want a schooner?"

"No, but a little thing like that won't hold the treasure; and even if it did, you can't go sailing about with a lot of gold vessels, and plates, and mitres, and things kicking about at the bottom of your boat."

"But you've not to seize the treasure, you know; all you have to do is to *find* it. The moment you are sure of it, you report the matter to the police, and leave the rest of the work to the lawyers."

To this there was no replying, so the rest of the conversation took a very practical turn. Digging materials were to be sent in the boat, wrapped up along with the mast, sail, rudder, and other parts of the boat's outfit. Mr. Griffins was very particular in laying down certain things that they were to be sure to do, and certain others that they were to be as sure not to do; but in their eagerness the lads gave him but scant attention. They had their own ideas about how to carry on a treasure-hunt, and were eager to put them into practice.

Great was their satisfaction when they found that, through the generosity of Uncle Roland, they were to have a certain amount of money each, as well as having their hotel bill paid; too much money, Mr. Griffins thought, but it was none of his business.

They were to start for Brendown next day at noon, and Mr. Griffins was to see them safely off. But they contrived to have a couple of hours to themselves before train time, while Mr. Griffins was at Houlston and Bamber's about the boat. This time they spent in hunting up a shop that Martin knew in the Strand, and there the three lads bought a revolver each—Martin had one already.

The others were content with elegant silver-mounted weapons that would go into the pocket; but Tony's heart was so completely won by a huge revolver in a handsome polished case, that he squandered nearly the whole of his allowance in acquiring it. As a matter of fact, he could hardly hold it out at arm's length, so heavy was it. But cost and weight were more than compensated for by its name; for the dealer showed the name printed inside the lid of the case—" Colt's Hair Trigger."

"It acks so quick, it'll bring down yer man afore 'e's time to get 'is 'and to 'is pocket," explained the dealer, to Tony's pride.

"Yes," added Wallace; "and then see the great advantage of this one. It's always ready; you don't even need to reach your pocket for *it*. You carry it over your shoulder, don't you, Tony?"

"Besides," struck in Ned, "see how useful it will be in our long boat. No need to take in ballast wi' that thing aboard. This hair trigger would trim a man-o'-war."

All the same, Tony paid his money and carried off

his boxful of revolver and appliances. Nor did they forget ammunition. If the railway company had known the contents of a certain rough deal box that the lads insisted upon having in the compartment with them, there certainly would have been trouble. But railway companies do not know everything; and even landladies have sometimes to be content with a certain area of ignorance in the wide sphere of their knowledge of the affairs of their guests.

Mrs. Peterson thought she knew all about the four young fellows who honoured the Victory Inn with their patronage, when she had pumped the innocent-looking Tony, and had ransacked Wallace's portmanteau, which happened to have the least formidable lock, and was accordingly entrusted with nothing but the most innocent underclothing. The four were set down as honest, hearty sailor lads out for a frolic.

The boat had arrived, bearing the unromantic name of the *Betsy Jane*, which, of course, was not to be tolerated; though there was at first a difficulty in selecting a name to satisfy everybody. As soon as the *Unicorn* was suggested, the discussion came to an abrupt end. It was felt that no improvement was possible, and Tony, as the neatest handed, was told off to paint in the name of Sir Walter's vessel.

A couple of days were spent in sailing about and getting the folks accustomed to the look of the *Unicorn*. Then it was proposed to have a night of it on the bay, and, like the thoughtful young fellows they were, our friends proposed to come home in the early morning; and to prevent annoyance to any one, they arranged to get to their rooms by means of a rope-ladder. There seemed no great necessity for this extreme care, as Mrs. Peterson was quite willing to leave the door unlocked all night; indeed, if the truth were known, it was seldom that her door was ever locked. Yet since they were sailor lads and fond of a frolic, nothing was thought of the arrangement; it seemed the most natural thing in the world.

CHAPTER XII.

THE PAINS OF TREASURE-HUNTING.

THE first visit to the abbey brought nothing but disappointment. Crossing the bay was delightful, and the boat was soon comfortably moored at a big stone in a creek that Ned knew well. It would not do to beach it, for they might have too far to haul it down to the water if the tide were ebbing; while if the tide were making, they ran the risk of having it carried off altogether. Tony, much against his will, was appointed sentinel at the boat, his instructions being to be prepared to put off at a moment's notice. The sail, the rudder, every rope and stick aboard, were arranged for immediate use, and each of the four knew exactly the part he would be expected to play should they have to set off in a hurry.

Crossing Mr. Brownjohn's outer wall was a perfect pleasure to folks who carried a rope-ladder with iron grapplings at the end. Martin carried a pick, Wallace a spade, while Ned carried an implement of which he did not know the name. It had a wooden shaft with a sharp iron end like a pick, and another bit of iron sticking out from it at right angles to the first. It was to be used to prize open the spaces between stones, and we may call it a lever.

Ned led his party straight to the treasure-corner. So far everything had gone well, but here they were made to realize, in a way they had never thought possible, what a noise a pick can make in the stillness of a clear night. The living part of the abbey was about two hundred yards from the remains of the chapel; but no sooner had Wallace struck a blow with his pick, than it became clear that it would be impossible to go on with the work without rousing the people in the house.

"Let's try, at any rate, whether there's a hollow sound over any of the stones," suggested Wallace.

Ned went about striking each of the stones in the suspected corner with his lever, while his companions followed him, disputing about the hollowness of the sounds. The truth was that none of them knew exactly the sort of sounds they wanted to hear. But they knew that they wanted to encourage Ned, so they stoutly maintained that the sounds were distinctly hollow.

The corner under which the treasure was supposed to lie had obviously once been a spiral staircase. Some of the broken steps lay around even yet, and the big round slab at the corner looked as if it had formerly formed the landing of the staircase.

"We needn't try to lift that stone," said Ned, tapping it with his lever; "but we can displace some of the little ones round about it, and see if it's hollow underneath. It's a good thing there are so many loose stones lying about anyway. It won't matter how we leave things; nobody'll suspect anything."

They worked on steadily with nothing but the lever, and the occasional help of the pick and the shovel used as levers. There was almost no sound, and almost as little result. At the end of an hour, however, they had got to the bottom of the round stone—that is, they had laid bare the thickness of this stone on one side. Their excitement may be imagined when they began to perceive that there was nothing under it. In other words, there was a vault or some kind of hole under the round slab. Of course this hole might be an ordinary part of the foundation, but the explorers naturally thought not.

Had they been able to use the pick freely, the mystery would have been soon solved; but as it was, they had to work slowly and painfully for another hour before they felt in a position to think of sending some one down to investigate further.

This critical moment was approaching. Every wrench of the lever was making the attempt more feasible, when suddenly the stillness was broken in the most appalling way.

There could be no mistaking it. What caused the three explorers to stop work was nothing other than a shot.

"It's Tony," cried Ned, throwing down his lever; "he's been attacked. Let's bolt."

"Steady!" cried Martin; "Tony's in no danger. He's done nothing against the law; we have. We've no time to lose, but we mustn't leave any traces here. Bring up some of those stones to cover up the hole, and all our implements as well."

Martin set himself to remove all traces of their night's work, and the others were not long in coming to his help. In less time than it takes to tell it affairs were restored to an appearance pretty much like what had prevailed before this incursion, and the three were at full speed for the boat.

On getting near the creek they began to move warily, in case they should run into a trap. But nothing whatever threatened. To their whispered cry, Tony answered that there was no danger now; so they sprang aboard, and had no difficulty in getting the *Unicorn* out into the bay. As soon as they felt themselves to be safe from pursuit, they turned to Tony for an explanation.

They found him in a state of total collapse.

"As share's onything, I didna mean tae dae it," he muttered, falling back upon his native Glasgow *patois;* and it took a great deal of coaxing and soothing to get anything like a connected account of what really had taken place.

After his friends had gone, Tony, not unnaturally, had become very uncomfortable. By-and-by he began to hear all manner of eerie sounds. The lapping of the water on the sides of the boat seemed magnified a thousandfold. Strange creakings and rustlings were heard on shore. Then a faint squeaking and tearing sound made itself heard. He had not been sure of the other sounds, but this one he was certain was not the result of his imagination. It was not. It was the sound of Ned's lever; but poor Tony did not know that.

It was after two hours of this had totally unnerved him that a distinct sound on shore attracted his attention, and glancing up quickly, he saw dimly against the black sky the body of a tall man.

"Is that you, Martin?" he chattered. But the dim figure made no reply. Then Tony had presented his revolver at the approaching figure, and plucking up his courage, demanded in his best tones,—

"Who goes there?"

Tony could not be sure whether the man answered or not. He thought he had begun to answer, but certainly no words reached Tony's ears; for the hair trigger had proved itself worthy of the name, and the revolver had gone off.

Tony was loud in his protestations that he had not meant to fire, but all felt that that would be a poor defence when he was tried for murder.

"But we did not come across any body when we came aboard," suggested Martin earnestly: "you may have missed."

"I don't think it," groaned Tony; "I heard moaning. I think he fell into the sea. I'm sure I heard a splash."

"Why didn't you tell us that before?" snarled Martin, now downright angry, for he well knew that as the eldest of the expedition all the blame would finally be laid at his door. "We might have been of some use to him if he wasn't killed outright. In fact, we'll better go back as it is."

"No, no—anything but that!" screamed Tony; "I can't go back there again."

But Martin was firm, and back they did go. It was a fruitless errand. Everything was as still as death. The shot seemed to have roused no attention. The dark lanterns they had brought with them were very useful, but nothing could be made out of the rocks or the shallow water.

"I shouldn't wonder if it was all Tony's imagination. He was in a blue funk, and didn't know what he was doing." So far Martin's words met with general approval, but his next were not so well received,—"What do you say to running back and finishing our job?"

The ominous silence which met this proposal was suddenly broken by Wallace, who had been plying his lantern on the rocks against which the boat was bumping.

"Oh, horror!"

He had put out his hand to shove off from the weed-covered rock, and had drawn it back covered with blood.

None of the others spoke or moved. Martin alone, with Wallace's bull's-eye, examined the rounded top of the bloodstained rock. Almost nothing could be seen against the dark green of the weed, but by touching it he made out that only a small portion retained the red stain.

"The tide's making now," said Martin slowly. "This stone is covered at high tide. There will be no trace to-morrow."

This was all the comfort to be had. The *Unicorn* was turned homewards. It was a silent voyage, and the four who clambered up their rope-ladder into their rooms were as miserable a quartet as England could have produced that night.

Tony and Ned shared the same room; Martin and Wallace had each a room.

"Don't go to bed!" pleaded Tony. "Or rather, come into my bed; I can't stand being alone. I say, you won't mind keeping in the lamp, eh?"

Ned had nothing to say. He wanted to blame Tony; but what would have been the good? Yet he could not find anything comforting to say; so he said nothing at all. Only he went over to Tony's bed—and somehow he was glad to go.

There they lay and shivered, and listened to the

hours striking on the impatient clock downstairs. Gradually the dawn came—cold, grey, deadly. The night was better than this. Without saying anything, Ned got up and blew out the lamp. Tony looked haggardly grateful.

Dawn was followed by a touch of red, and soon the sun's first rays fell aslant the bed.

"Tell me it's a dream, Ned; it *can't* be true."

Ned frowned. He did not like this silliness. How could he say it wasn't true when he knew it was true, and Tony too? At his friend's frown poor Tony shrivelled up.

It was half-past seven before either spoke again. This time it was Ned.

"We must get up, Tony. There's no good lying here. It'll only draw attention to us."

"What's the good of getting up? I can't go down to breakfast. O Ned, what a face you've got!"

"If it's anything like yours, it's a caution to snakes," cried Ned, springing up; and then, after seeing his face in the mirror, cried in dismay, "We can't appear with faces like these. I wonder what a bath—"

But at this moment there was a noisy entrance of some people by the front door below, some loud talking, a clatter of boots on the stair, and a hammering at the door.

"Open, in the Queen's name!" shouted a hoarse voice.

Tony, who had been resting on his elbow, fell back upon the pillow. Ned, after a second crash at the door, went forward and unlocked it. To his great surprise and intense relief, Martin and Wallace bounced in, radiant. Tapping Ned on the shoulder, Wallace began,—

"I arrest you in—"

But a sight of Ned's face stopped all buffoonery.

"I say, Ned, it's all right. Nobody's killed or even injured. It's all a mistake.—Cheer up, Tony!"

But Tony did not find it easy to cheer up at a moment's notice. In the meantime, at any rate, he was unconscious; the shock, following on a night of agony, had been too much for him. It took the others a good ten minutes' work to bring him round, and then it took all their care to prevent him from going off again. By-and-by he became calm enough to listen to Martin's explanation.

Wallace and he had not wanted to go to bed, had not wanted even to go each to his own room. Martin had asked Wallace to come into his room, and there they had talked over the whole situation, and gradually come to the conclusion that they had acted very badly in not giving the alarm. The man might only have been wounded, and might have gone off to some little distance, and there dropped from loss of blood.

"He may be lying somewhere bleeding to death at this very moment," muttered Martin, "and nobody can find him for hours yet."

"Is it too late to go back, after all?" ventured Wallace, whose conscience was as hard worked as Martin's.

"I think not," was the nervous reply. "There's nothing to hinder us scudding across the bay. The wind's all right. But, I say, let's go by ourselves. The youngsters are not fit to face up this thing; but we should be able—we *must* be able!"

Prompt action followed; in a few minutes they were once more on their way across the bay. Dawn was now breaking, and when they landed at the scene of the tragedy, there was light enough to guide them over the rocks. The tide was nearly full, and the rounded rock that had shown the fatal stain was now no longer to be seen. Clambering over the wet sea-weed that covered the remaining rocks, neither

Wallace nor Martin could discover anything out of the common.

They had searched all round for three-quarters of an hour, and the light was now bright enough for them to see everything quite clearly. Wallace was sticking to the rocks, while Martin was moving inland, making for the coast road, when Wallace gave a shout that brought his friend to his side in a few moments.

Martin's first idea was that Wallace had lost his head through the excitement of the night's work, for he stood on the smooth, sloping face of a rock and capered about like a monkey. On coming closer, the young officer was confirmed in his belief when he found the rock stained with blood. But Wallace soon settled the matter by pointing to a dark mass at the bottom of the slope, and yelling,—

"There's the corpse of Wedgeworth's man!"

A glance was enough. There lay a goat in a perfect pool of blood. Martin's first feeling was one of intense relief, then of languid surprise.

"I didn't think a goat had so much blood in its ugly body."

"You don't imagine that it shed all that pool, do you?" cried Wallace gleefully. "Why, don't you see that it has only tinted the water in the pool! That pool's there as a steady thing, I wager."

"Does the tide reach the pool?" asked Martin anxiously.

"It must," replied Wallace, peering into the discoloured water to see what sort of animals it contained. "Yes, yes, it does. It'll be touch and go, though. But—yes; it will get in by this fissure here."

By this time they had managed to scramble down beside the goat, though at great risk of a red ducking, the thought of which neither of them relished. The body was still warm, and they could not be quite sure whether the animal was dead or not.

"We can't leave it here," said Martin, "for this bullet-hole in the neck would tell tales that we don't want told."

"We can't drop it into the water here either, for it would just drift ashore. We must carry it round to our boat, and drop it overboard in the middle of the bay."

A few minutes afterwards the two were exchanging opinions on the weight of goats, each admitting that up till that moment he had done great injustice to the weight of the average dead goat.

Arrived at the boat, panting and a little out of temper with the heavy load, Martin objected to take the filthy thing aboard and make a mess of everything.

"We don't want the *Unicorn* to come home covered with gore. Let's take the brute in tow, drag him out to the middle of the bay, and settle his hash with one or two of those big stones. They'll maybe help him to keep his place—at the bottom."

Wallace knew from personal experience that animals disposed of in this way have a habit of rising again in spite of stones or other anchors. But it takes a little time for such enterprising corpses to reduce their specific gravity to floating-point, and by that time the work at Arnwyke would be over.

Finally everything was neatly and comfortably arranged and carried out, and the two overjoyed young men arrived at the inn in such good spirits as almost to frighten Tony to death. They had no idea how far the boy had been run down by his fearful night, or they would have acted otherwise. As it was, they did their best to make up for the harm they had done. Tony was kept in bed, reported to Mrs. Peterson as ill, and Ned was told off to attend him. Wallace and Martin themselves lounged about most of the day on the sofa and easy-chair (time about), and went early to bed.

Next morning the four were practically all right again, and Tony was eager to go on with the excavations. He was ready to do anything to show that he was not really a coward, so long as manslaughter was kept out of the business.

"It wasn't fear that was the matter with me," he protested; "it was the thought of having killed a man. None of you fellows knows what that means. I didn't till the night before last. I think, on the whole, I'd rather be killed than kill anybody."

"Don't worry about it," said Martin uneasily. "We were all in a pretty blue funk, I take it, and the less said the sooner mended. Are we ready for the abbey to-night?"

"Yes; but it's not my turn to watch this time," demurred Tony.—" Will you watch to-night, Ned?"

"Ned can't," remonstrated Martin. "Don't you see *he* must find the treasure? But Wallace will watch—eh, Wallace? You're not afraid, eh?"

"Not much," was the sarcastic reply; but, all the same, Wallace thought they might at least have tossed for it.

Nothing special happened on the next voyage

across. Wallace duly took his post as sentinel in the boat, and the other three set to work. After two hours' hard labour (for they found that they had not done so much as they had thought at their first visit), they had made a sufficiently wide opening in the side of the cylindrical cavity under the staircase to allow of one of them getting through with ease.

Peering down the hole, they could make nothing of it, except that it looked like a funnel or a well. Ned dropped a stone into the funnel, and heard it strike something hard in a twinkling.

"It isn't very deep," said Martin, "and that's a good thing; and it isn't a well, which is a better thing. For, to tell the truth, that's what I've been afraid of since we discovered this hole. But it's evidently not a well, or, at any rate, if it is, it's a dry one."

This last remark was one of those cautious sayings that treasure-hunting encourages. In this business you're never quite sure of anything.

"What an abominable smell!" cried Tony. "I wonder if it's poisonous."

All three drew back instinctively, and Ned asked what he meant. Then it came out that Tony was basing his fears upon a story current among his schoolfellows in Glasgow, that there was a secret passage from Glasgow Cathedral to Edinburgh Castle, but it was filled with poisonous gas, and nobody could use it now.

"They say that the last man who went in at Edinburgh was a piper with his dog. He went in playing, 'Will ye no come back again?' and he never came out."

"And what about the dog?" asked Martin, wiping his brow, for he had done most of the lever work this time.

"Oh, *it* came out at Glasgow right enough, but it had no skin on it; and they say—"

"Stow that, you gruesome fellow! I feel my own skin getting tight. Let's try a light. If a light burns steady, then it's all right. A man can live wherever a candle can burn brightly."

This final statement is not quite accurate, but it has more truth in it than treasure-seekers are accustomed to. They were getting the lantern ready to lower with the door open, when Tony again interrupted,—

"Maybe the light will explode the gas."

"You miserable little croaker," growled Martin, "I'll wring your wretched little neck if you give us any more of your cheerful tittle-tattle. Stand by to lower the lantern there!"

The three eagerly watched the light slowly descending, peeping timidly at first down the hole in momentary expectation of an explosion, but soon gaining confidence. The light burned cheerfully all the way; apparently all was safe. Further, the depth was very little greater than the length of the rope-ladder.

"Volunteers for the hole!" cried Martin, looking pointedly at Ned, who quietly agreed to make the descent.

The reader is probably unaware how extremely unpleasant it is to go down a rope-ladder with nobody to hold the foot of it. Add to this inconvenience possibilities of explosion and poisoning and total ignorance of where you are going, and you have some notion of what Ned felt as he went down that hole. Martin had insisted upon the further precaution of tying a rope round Ned's waist, and fastening it to one of the huge blocks of stone lying at the mouth of the hole. This was to meet the case of there being no proper support at the end of the ladder.

By-and-by a ghostly whisper came up from the depths, to the great relief of the two above,—

"All right; I'm in a passage. I'm loosing the rope."

For maybe five minutes there were darkness and silence below—five minutes that seemed interminable to the two watchers. Then Ned's lantern appeared again, and another ghostly whisper came up,—

"I'm going to try the other end of the passage," and again the light disappeared.

By-and-by the light reappeared once more, and this time Ned mounted the ladder.

"Well, what sign of the treasure?" asked Martin eagerly.

"None at all," said Ned, a little disconsolately; "but we are not going to give up yet."

"We'll need to make off for to-night, anyhow," broke in Tony, who had a fellow-feeling for the distant sentinel; "Wallace will be in a dreadful funk by this time."

"You're right. Let's cover up our work as well as possible, and make off."

It took about a quarter of an hour to remove all traces of their work, and then they made for the *Unicorn*. As soon as they had put off, Ned explained all that he had discovered.

"The first way I went, to the left, just led to a

dead wall. I hit it and kicked it, but it didn't sound the least hollow."

"Was the passage high enough for you to walk in, or had you to creep?"

"I could walk quite easily; but the air was awful—it made me quite sick."

Here Wallace turned his dark lantern on Ned's face, which certainly corroborated what he had said.

"And at the other end?" put in Tony.

"The other end comes to a staircase that goes both up and down—a very narrow spiral staircase. I went up; but there were only thirteen steps altogether, and then the whole thing stops. It runs into the roof, and stops there. The last step forms part of the roof."

"Did you try down too?" asked Martin, with a good deal of sympathy in his tone. He seemed to guess that it was all over with the treasure.

"Yes, I went down," said Ned slowly, "and very nearly came to my death. As I went down I was counting the steps. Next time I go down I must take a bull's-eye; it lights up where you're going, and leaves your eyes in the dark. My lantern dazzled me a little, and it was a mere chance that I noticed that the seventeenth step was missing."

"Why the seventeenth?"

"How should I know? All I know is that at the fifteenth step I lifted the lantern above my head, and saw in front of me nothing but blackness. Looking down at my feet, I saw there was one step more, and then none—nothing but blackness there too."

"But what was above you?"

"Nothing but blackness too."

"Do you mean to say that the world came to an end down there at the foot of that stair?" asked Martin, trying to rouse Ned out of his state of horror.

"Not the end of the world, only the end of the stair, and very nearly the end of me."

"We must go down, the whole three of us, to-morrow night, and see what we can make of it. We'll take down some stones, and chuck them off the end of the world, and see how far they'll go."

"And we'll take dark lanterns," added Ned grimly.

"The stair that stopped at the roof, what do you make of it?" asked Tony.

"How far up did it go, Ned?" asked Martin; "half-way up to the surface?"

"A little more, I think."

"So there must be something like six or eight feet

at least of solid mason-work between the end of your stair and the surface. No wonder we could hear no hollow sound."

"But, you see, there is nearly a fathom of building and earth and stones over our hole itself," commented Ned; "so we needn't be surprised at what has happened to the top of the staircase."

"How does this strike you?" put in Wallace. "The corner is evidently the place where Sir Walter meant us to enter right enough. That staircase must have been in existence in his time, with a proper outlet. Somebody discovered the staircase, helped himself to the treasure, and built up the staircase for ever."

"Striking and even probable, Wallace; but I cannot say it is very encouraging," added Martin.

"But, in that case, what is the meaning of that broken staircase? where did it use to go to? Maybe the treasure's down at the foot, where that lower stair used to go to."

"At any rate," concluded Ned, "it isn't time to knuckle down yet; there's a lot to be seen still in that old hole."

In this, at least, the others agreed, and all looked forward with eagerness to the discoveries of the next visit.

CHAPTER XIII.

THE WEASELS JOIN IN.

THE next night was clear and starry—so clear, indeed, that Martin was unwilling to start.

"You might as well go by daylight," he said.

But the eagerness of the others was too much for him; they set off as before. Tony this time volunteered to keep the boat while the others explored. Everybody was anxious to be in at the death, so this was considered very handsome of Tony, though his real reason was to show that his character for pluck was well earned. He wanted the others to forget his former fright.

This time both Martin and Ned went into the passage, Wallace keeping guard outside. They went first to the staircase end, and carefully examined it. There was nothing to remark except a couple of strong wooden beams just under the place where the steps ended above—that is, just under the place where the staircase had been built up. Between the strong beams were the remains of certain smaller pieces of wood.

"What would you say that means?" asked Martin, pointing to the wood.

"I can't say; have you an idea?"

"It seems to me pretty plain that this staircase has been built in *from the outside*. This wood was to give the stones time to set. You see they make a groined arch, which could not have been made without woodwork; but a groined arch, once it is made, is so strong that you could safely build a tower on it."

"And what is your idea about the lower stair, in that case?"

"Let's go and see it first."

Standing on the lowest step, and flashing their bull's-eyes into the darkness, they fancied that they made out dim outlines somewhere in front of them. When a stone was cast downwards, it rattled irregularly against something, evidently at no great distance. A stone cast violently right ahead struck against something, and evidently rebounded, reaching the ground almost immediately.

"We've evidently not quite got to the end of the

world yet," said Martin cheerily. "What do you say to a swing down here? I'd like to go myself; but you could never pull me up again if anything went wrong, while I think I could drag you up. It's too deep for the ladder, I'm afraid. You must go down hand over hand, but that won't bother you."

Ned peered into the black abyss uneasily, and said nothing. He was not exactly afraid, but he certainly would have liked it better had he known exactly what sort of danger he was running into.

"I'll tell you what I'll do," said Martin. "I'll fasten the end of the rope to one of those beams up there, and go down myself. I'll easily manage to get up hand over hand."

"I wasn't funking, Mr. Martin," said Ned guiltily; "I was only calculating the risk. But we'll fasten the rope as you say, all the same; it'll be safer."

The beam proved to be as solid as the day it was placed there, and afforded a capital hold for the rope. It is true that the rope made two turns of the staircase before it reached the final step; but it was a long rope, and there was quite enough of it, for the end evidently reached something below. Martin insisted upon tying the rope round Ned's waist, in case anything should happen; and Ned, in turn, insisted upon Martin's tying a short rope round his own waist and fastening the other end round the second beam. In this way the third mate was able to reach the final step, but could not get much further; so that if his foot slipped he could only fall perhaps a couple of feet, and could easily regain his footing by the help of the rope.

Ned was let down very slowly by his friend. It was a big strain on Martin paying out the rope so gradually, while it was not pleasant for Ned to be spinning slowly round and round like a fowl before a fire. Sooner than either had expected the ground was reached. At all events, something was reached on which Ned could stand, for the strain on the rope suddenly ceased.

Flashing his bull's-eye about him, Ned found that he was standing on the top of a heap of broken stones, which he had no difficulty in recognizing as the *débris* of the staircase that ended so suddenly above. As far as the rays of his lantern could carry, he saw broken stones, but the main mass was gathered together into the heap on which he stood.

Clambering down from his heap, he found himself in a spacious cave, for the walls of this strange place were evidently natural and not built. He quickly made the tour of it, but found no appearance of any outlet. The walls were wet, with here and there some ugly, slimy green stuff growing on them. There was nothing else of any interest.

It was an easy matter getting up again to Martin's level; and it was well that they had not waited much longer, for Wallace was in a very anxious state when they signalled him.

"Have you got anything? I thought you were dead," he whispered down.

"Hold on for a minute," was the reply; "we are going to see how the other end looks."

Arrived there, they soon made up their minds that the passage had been simply built up. The roof, which was arched all the way, was not fitted to the ending wall—the wall was fitted to it; and though there was no hollow sound in answer to their tappings, they were not surprised at that, since they knew the extreme thickness of the masonry elsewhere.

"Our hope certainly lies here, Ned," said Martin.

Ned made no reply; he was trying to plan out in his own mind the lie of the well-known secret passage in which he had so often played as a boy.

"I'm afraid it's all up now," he said. "I'm almost sure that this passage is nothing but a continuation of one that we used to play in. The passage on the other side leads into the cloisters, and I have the best of reasons for knowing that there is no treasure there."

"All the same, we must break through and see," was Martin's cheery answer. "Why, there's probably six or eight feet of stone between the two passages, and what is more likely than that the treasure is just between these passages?"

But in spite of the free use of pick and lever—for no sound could be heard from above likely to disturb any one—they had made but little progress when it was time to return to Brendown.

This time the watching had told more on Wallace than on Tony. For Tony had spent the time fishing, and had had good luck. The inn people had thought it remarkable, and not unreasonably, that for two whole nights they should have fished and caught nothing. Tony had put this all right now.

Next night Wallace was fisherman, and Tony was to be sentinel at the entrance to the cave. Martin and Ned had agreed that the lower cave should be thoroughly explored before any more time was wasted over the solid masonry at the end of the passage, which, after all, might only lead straight into the well-known part of the abbey passages.

"This cave seems to have had two entrances in its day, both now blocked up," said Tony oracularly.

"But why?" asked Martin; "that's what we want to be at."

"Let's go down and see," said Tony—"let's all go down. There's no good keeping a watch here at the mouth. We can easily climb up again by the help of the block and tackle we have brought."

Emboldened by their previous freedom from interruption, all three did go down, leaving the entrance to look after itself. Martin was very anxious to go down himself into the lower cave, but felt it to be his duty to remain as before on the final step, to make sure of securing the return of his fellows. Both ropes had been left attached to the beams, and were now called into requisition. Martin was once more moored to the beam by the smaller rope, and first Ned and then Tony swung his way into the depths beneath.

It soon became clear that two explorers were better than one. At one of the angles of the cave Tony discovered a triangular slit, narrow at the top but fairly wide at the bottom. The bull's-eyes, when turned into the hole, showed that it did not go far back; and after a little peering, the boys made out what they thought to be the beginning of a flight of steps.

Ned looked at the hole, then at Tony. Tony looked at Ned, then at the hole. The measurement was done with the eye, and not a word was spoken. Yet both understood that as Tony was much the smaller it fell to him to continue the exploration on the other side of that narrow opening.

"I think I can manage to squeeze through," said Tony doubtfully, as he stooped down to try. It cost a good deal of scraping and puffing, but it was managed at last, much more easily than had been expected.

From the other side Tony explained how you had only to twist your right leg under your left, and that let you have the advantage of the hollow in the ground under the opening, and you could glide through like winking. On the whole, Ned thought it wise to decline Tony's invitation to follow him; it would be safer to have one on each side.

"Hand me through my bull's-eye, then," whispered Tony, though there was no need of whispering, "and keep your one shining through the hole to guide me back."

"All right, Tony; I won't budge. Keep your pecker up."

But Ned soon found that his own pecker was inclined to descend. There was something eerie in listening to the very deliberate footsteps of his companion as they grew fainter and fainter. Tony was evidently off on a long journey.

Ned was glad that Martin was in sight up there, with his ship's lantern waving in his hand, halfway up the left-hand wall. Leaving his bull's-eye shining through the hole, as a sort of lighthouse to insure his friend's return, Ned went over and reported progress to Martin, who was so excited with the news that he wanted to come down at once to help. While they were discussing the advisability of his coming down, they were interrupted by a faint shriek that seemed to come from the bottom of the earth, but which they both rightly thought to be from Tony. Ned darted away, and Martin was preparing to unlash himself from his rope, when he felt himself seized roughly from behind, and heard a gruff voice say something about the Queen.

But the gruff voice got no further than the beginning of its loyal speech. The owner of the voice, however, did get a bit further; for in throwing himself upon Martin he had thrust him over the last step, and sent him spinning into empty space. He of the gruff voice was unable to pull himself up in time, but as he fell he made a grab at Martin's legs, which were swung back at that moment. This grab probably saved the gruff one's life, for it broke the fall very considerably.

There was a dull thud, then a moment of absolute stillness and darkness; for Martin's lantern had been knocked out of his hand, and by this time Ned's bull's-eye was on the other side of the triangular opening along with Ned himself, who, all unconscious of this outside attack, had hastened to apply Tony's twist of the right leg under the left, in order to get through to the relief of Tony himself.

Trying in vain to get a footing on the step, and condemning his own carelessness in having taken too great a length of rope for his present comfort, Martin was surprised to see a light appear round the upper turn of the stair, and to hear a stern voice demanding,—

"Parsons, are you there? Unless we get an answer at once we fire."

"Hold hard!" yelled Martin, struggling to get a footing, but finding his movements greatly interfered with by the pressure of his whole weight on the rope under his armpits. "Don't shoot, or you'll be sorry for it. Your Parsons has broken his neck, I daresay." Here Martin's voice rose to a scream,—"Hold on, you blockhead! keep back, or you'll be after him."

The warning was barely in time, for Lieutenant Rankler, revolver in hand, was now on the second last step. For a moment he stood gazing at the dangling figure before him; but Martin brought him to his senses by exclaiming,—

"Grab that rope to your left, and give me a lift up. This rope's longer than I bargained for. And, oh, I say, if it's all the same to you, I'd like you to turn that revolver some other way; it might go off."

"But it isn't all the same to me," answered the other grimly, as he gave Martin a gentle shove which just prevented his finding a footing and sent him spinning off again. "And it certainly may go off."

"Oh, I say, look here," cried Martin, a little out of breath from his exertions in his remarkable position, "what do you mean?"

"Where's the bo'sun?" asked Rankler sternly.

"If you mean the man who tried to throttle me," puffed Martin, "he's down there among a heap of stones. I hope he hasn't knocked his brains out."

"You may well hope that, my man; for if he has, your swinging will require to be continued at an early date—with a trifling difference."

"If *I* were anxious about the health of a man down there," retorted Martin, with as much dignity as he could throw into his dance upon nothing, "I think I'd go down to look after him, instead of bullying a poor fellow whose life is being squeezed out of him up here."

"How many men have you down there?" asked Rankler, admitting the truth of Martin's remonstrance, but yet unwilling to risk an ambush.

"There are no men, only two lads. But hurry, man, if you wish to help your bo'sun. Gi' me a lift up."

This time Martin got the lift, and in a trice he had shown the lieutenant the rope by which Ned and Tony had gone down.

"It's not deep," remarked Martin encouragingly.

"You go first, Dunsburn," said the lieutenant; "and if any attempt is made on you, I'll shoot this fellow like a dog."

This was said very loudly, partly to impress Martin, but more for the benefit of the supposed desperadoes below. Martin only smiled. In a very few minutes half a dozen man-o'-war's men and their lieutenant were standing round Parsons, doing their best to bring him round.

The man's right knee was a little out of working order, but all the rest of him seemed to have escaped. He appeared to relish the brandy that was swung down to him from some friend on the broken stair.

"And now, my fine fellow," said Rankler, turning to Martin, "we'll go into your affairs, if you please."

"At your service, sir," replied Martin, saluting.

"May I ask what you are doing? But, I say, I thought you told me you had two accomplices; where are they?"

Here the lieutenant got into a state, for no trace of any one, boy or man, was to be seen.

"If they have escaped, my man, you'll pay for it. What fools we were to make such a fuss about Parsons, while those fellows were making off! But where did they go?"

"There's a cleft in the wall at that corner," replied Martin politely. "One of the boys went through it just before Parsons attacked me; the other seems to have followed him."

In a twinkling the group had gathered round the triangular opening, and reminded Martin of nothing so much as a meeting of terriers round a rat-hole. The leanest among them could not hope to squeeze through, yet it seemed too humiliating to wait there till the rats chose to come out. Martin put down his head to the hole and bellowed,—

"Ne-e-e-e-d!"

"Ay, ay, sir," came the reply from quite close at hand. "He's fainted, and I've no brandy."

"Who's fainted?" asked Rankler, as he handed the brandy-flask to Martin, not without a doubtful shake, to see if perchance Parsons had left any.

"It's the other fellow," replied Martin, as he stooped down to pass the flask through the hole to Ned, who came down the steps to receive it. Then noticing that his explanation did not seem quite to satisfy the lieutenant, he went on: "Wedgeworth is the little one. He's not very strong, and is always getting into mischief. He shouldn't be on an expedition like this at all."

"Amen to that. Now that we have a little time while our friends are doctoring each other, I shall be glad if you will tell me exactly what this expedition of yours *is*. I may say that we have secured your boat and the pretended fisherman."

"Oh, Wallace," replied Martin indifferently, willing to gain time.

"To the point," said Rankler sternly. "What are you doing here? I have the right to ask."

"Yes, yes; I can read," retorted Martin, irritably gazing at the "H.M.S. *Weasel*" on one of the men's caps.

"Well, can't you speak as well?"

Martin had never realized till that moment how extremely foolish treasure-hunting must seem to the impartial outsider. He found it impossible to say straight out to those common-sense men what had brought him and his companions there.

"Well, if I must speak, I may as well admit that we have come here on what seems to me now very much like a wild-goose chase."

Rankler only looked patient, waiting for more information. Martin had to go on.

"To tell the truth, we came here treasure-hunting."

"That I believe; but what is your special fancy in treasures—silks, or brandy?"

"Oh no," replied Martin, with a sigh of relief;

"you're quite at sea there. The Queen—God bless her—has no account against us. It's a family treasure."

Here Ned made a welcome diversion by calling through the hole that Tony had recovered, and was going to try to wriggle his way back. In a very short time his pale, haggard face was being carefully scanned under the glare of two ship lanterns. Ned's face, when he joined the group, was hardly less ghastly than Tony's.

"Why, what's the matter?" cried Ned, as soon as he had recovered, to some small extent, from his astonishment at the change that had taken place in the cave since he had quitted it a few minutes before. "Where have all those fellows come from?"

"It's your place to answer questions, my lad, not to ask them."

It was Rankler who made this remark; but before he had time to get an answer, Martin struck in,—

"Yes, Ned, he's all right. They're from H.M.S. *Weasel*. Now tell me what you saw in there. Have you found anything?"

"But what do the Weasels want here?"

"I say, will you answer? Have you hurt yourself, or did Tony?"

"Oh no; I didn't hurt myself. And as to what we saw, ask him."

"You tell, Ned; I *can't*."

Thus driven to the point, Ned told how he had squeezed through the hole as soon as he had heard the shriek, and had stumbled up the stairs and along a long gallery that was very narrow though fairly high. There was only the one way possible, so he had no fear either of missing Tony or of losing his way back. He had pushed on unhesitatingly, keeping the light of his bull's-eye steadily on the ground in case of a hole; for his fear had been that Tony had tumbled down some such hole. Soon this fear for Tony was set at rest; for there he lay in a heap before him, and beside him lay the extinguished bull's-eye, giving out its usual unpleasant stench.

Busy with his efforts to rouse Tony, he had paid no attention to anything else. It was not till he had returned with the brandy, and had given Tony some, that he had time to look around. His first glance nearly laid him out beside his friend; for there in the corner sat a grinning skeleton, apparently watching him.

At this point Ned felt that he had a right to a pull at the brandy on his own account. The spirit put enough courage into him to enable him to turn once more to the corner. He was not mistaken. There lay, or rather sat, the skeleton, with a piece of armour resting on its knees, while a steel cap lay at a little distance off.

By this time, too, he was able to see that the passage seemed to end here; but he could not make any more detailed examination, for Tony had so far recovered as to be able to travel along the passage with Ned's help. They reached the hole—and that was all.

"Where does the passage lead to, do you think?" asked Martin.

"I can't say. I did not think of the passage at all," was Ned's irritated reply. Tony had more information.

"It looks as if it went to the sea, for before I saw *him* I thought I heard the splashing of water."

Here Rankler took command again.

"All this is very fine, very romantic, no doubt; but I want to know more about this treasure business. Whose treasure is it supposed to be?"

In as few words as possible Martin gave the requisite information. Rankler seemed half inclined to believe the tale, but his decision was not at all affected by that.

"In any case you three have got to come aboard

the *Weasel* till we get to the bottom of this business—you and the fellow in the boat. I can't say that I like the look of things."

At this point a sailor stepped forward and saluted.

"Well, Briggs, what now?"

"B'pardon, sir, but this young gen'leman is the old squire's son, Mas'er Ned Campadder."

"Eh, what? Well, what's that got to do with this business?"

"Well, sir, there be a story o' some treasure i' the family, sir, an' maybe it's all right. I didn' know 'e was one o' them, or I wouldn' 'ave reported 'em."

Rankler obviously softened at this, and it soon came out that Briggs, the coastguardsman, had heard about the nightly fishings—with no fish to show for them—of those strangers at the inn. Their nautical appearance had roused his suspicions, and he had watched their proceedings on the previous night. An unexplained rumour of the sound of firearms had reached his ears too. Altogether everything looked suspicious enough to warrant him in sending word to the revenue cutter *Weasel*, with the result that we know.

"If you'd on'y 'a trusted yer ole frien', Mas'er Ned, you'd 'ave 'ad my 'elp, not my 'indrance, and them honest lads 'ad 'a bin sleepin' i' their bunks at this minnit."

"I had to find the treasure myself," explained Ned, lamely enough. But it was manifestly impossible to enter into legal questions with a straightforward coastguardsman.

Turning next to the officer, he said,—

"You'll bear me witness, sir, won't you, that I discovered this hiding-place first; and if any treasure is found in it, it's mine, isn't it?"

"As to that I can't say," replied Rankler. "All I know is that we found you here, and that you say there's a skeleton through that hole. I confess that I think the smuggling idea is played out. But you must come with me to the *Weasel* to-night, all the same. The whole thing's too suspicious."

And to the *Weasel* they had to go; not, however, before Martin had persuaded the Weasels to take a careful look round, and to promise to bring the necessary implements next day, if their commander permitted, for a complete search.

CHAPTER XIV.

BROWNJOHN RAGES—MARTIN WINKS.

IT was on the forenoon of the fourth day after Rankler's appearance in the Arnwyke vaults—for business of this kind cannot be hurried, and demands some correspondence that goes post free—that Mr. Brownjohn received by messenger a big yellow envelope, on which were printed, above his own name, the words, "On Her Majesty's Service." So far this was very pleasant; he swelled with pride as he broke the opulent red seal. But he immediately afterwards swelled with anger. It was an intimation that the vaults of the abbey were to be searched that day for contraband articles.

In a furious temper Mr. Brownjohn threw on his hat, and dashed down the avenue to the main entrance to give orders to the lodge-keeper to admit no man, whether he wore the Queen's uniform or not, till a regular search-warrant was produced. The yellow letter seemed a sort of a warrant too, it is true, but it was not the kind of warrant with which the old gentleman was familiar. He was a justice of the peace, and if he didn't know about warrants, who did?

As a matter of fact, Mr. Brownjohn's ideas of the law on this subject were of the vaguest, and, if they had been analyzed, would have shown themselves to be based on nothing but the strong conviction that an Englishman's house is his castle; and if that is true of an ordinary house in a street, how much more must it be true of a house that is shut in on all sides by a ten-foot wall? His orders showed that he contemplated something in the nature of a siege.

"Keep the gate locked, and on no account—"

"It's too late, sir," pleaded the old door-keeper; "the lieutenant and his men went in with the letter to you, sir."

A little time was wasted by Mr. Brownjohn in explaining how little he thought of the gate-keeper; but the old servant wisely directed his master's anger elsewhere by indicating the direction taken by the blue-jackets.

Seven minutes afterwards, Mr. Brownjohn stood puffing in imminent danger of apoplexy, gaping at a sailor who was leaning on a gun mounted with a sword-bayonet, at the corner where our friends had made the hole into the vaults.

"Hullo, you, where's the other blackguards?"

"Meanin'?" asked the sailor politely. He had been warned by Briggs of what was likely to happen, and had been tutored by that wily coastguardsman how to treat the dangerous justice of the peace.

"Folks as 'as lots o' frien's in parlyment mustn' be 'ustled. The commander 'as got all th' papers right, an' no objecshuns can be 'ad agin 'em; but if we do the least thin' ayon' our billet, there'll be wot they calls a queshun i' th' 'Ouse. I dunno dzackly wot that is, but it's summat the commander 'ates like pison. So you min's yer P's an' Q's."

Accordingly, when the justice of the peace went on to ask in the most insolent way, "Where's your master?" Jack proceeded to mind his P's and Q's by holding his tongue, and with aggravating complacency jerking his thumb over his shoulder in the direction of the hole, which now appeared black and clear in the daylight.

For a moment Mr. Brownjohn could not believe his eyes. He had been told at the gate that nearly twenty men all told had come in, and here was only one left. The rest—if this ruffian with the gun was to be believed—had disappeared mysteriously into the ground through a hole the existence of which he had never even suspected.

Approaching to peer into the hole, the old gentleman was exasperated to find that the sailor had unostentatiously interposed his body.

"Get out of my way, you jackanapes!" cried the ill-natured old man.

"My orders is to shoot any one 'oo interferes wi' me in the discharge o' my dooty. But I'll make a exception o' an ole man like you. 'Cos w'y? Ye *can't* interfere, d'ye see? Ye 'aven't the fightin' weight, cap'n."

This was too much. Down came Mr. Brownjohn's cane, with all the frosty strength left in him, on the sentinel's mid thigh.

Jack now found himself very unhappily placed. It is difficult managing one's P's and Q's under circumstances like these. You may have a gun, and a bayonet too; but if your opponent knows that you cannot really use them, it puts you at a disadvantage. Besides, if you are a sturdy young sailor man just turned thirty, you cannot, with any decency, catch a surly old pantaloon by the neck and shake him like a rat, as you would like to.

All the same, you cannot stand by and be flogged like a disobedient puppy, and there isn't anything really to prevent you grounding arms on the old gentleman's toes; while, if the old gentleman happens to have corns, why, that's his affair. This, at least, was how it struck Jack, with the result that the encounter became much more equal.

When the old gentleman had finished his dance, and had returned to the attack, demanding admission to his own hole, and that immediately, Jack had recovered his temper enough to take up a light tone.

"If I was to do the proper thing by ye, I'd let ye go in at your own 'ole an' drop down an' break your own neck. It's easy done: a ten-foot drop's good enough for your age an' build."

Mr. Brownjohn's reply was quite up to standard, and poor Jack began to perceive that in a war of words he was not likely to shine. So knowing from Briggs what a money-grub the old fellow was, he thought he would keep up his end of the argument by twitting the old man with the treasure below.

The effect was not at all what the sailor had expected. Instead of being driven to desperation by the thought of the money he was likely to let slip through his fingers, Mr. Brownjohn became distinctly calmer—too calm, in fact; for the change was so great as to call back to Jack's mind the strict orders he had had to mention the treasure to no one.

It was in vain that Brownjohn now tried to pump the sentinel as to who exactly were down below. Were they all sailors, or was there a civilian among them? Jack shook his head. Had any lawyer anything to do with the case? Jack was obdurate.

Things seemed to have come pretty much to a deadlock. Jack was busy lamenting his folly in having let the cat out of the bag, while Brownjohn was as busy considering ways and means of turning to his own profit the information he had just received. The strain of the position was relieved in a startling way. A sudden and terrible rumbling was heard from below, and in a moment or two a cloud of dense white smoke came puffing out of the hole which Jack was guarding.

"Oh, what's that?" exclaimed the old gentleman.

"If ye ax me," replied Jack darkly, "I'd say 'twas a earthquake. An' if ye takes my advice, ye'll make yerself scarce. Ye're mighty well off t' be able t' go. Look at me, waitin' 'ere till I'm blowed up."

Maybe Mr. Brownjohn did feel a little unsafe in this mysterious part of his estate; maybe he felt that he was wasting time trying to pump this dry well of a sentinel. In any case, he made off post-haste to his lawyers, to see what they had to say on this interesting subject; while Jack remained behind, wondering whether very much harm had been done by his careless speech.

The cause of the explosion has no doubt been already guessed. The explorers wished to get into the gallery where the skeleton was, and since even twisting the right leg under the left was hopeless for grown men, they determined to blast the big stone that blocked the way.

Before applying the gunpowder, however, they had satisfied themselves that the obstructing stone had fallen in from the side for some reason, and had thus closed a passage otherwise meant to be open. The *Weasel's* doctor, who knew a little about most things, said it was clear that the opening had been originally partly natural and partly artificial, and that the artificial part had not been very well done; hence the collapse.

A comparatively small charge was used, but the result in sound and smoke in that confined space was much more than any one there had expected. It was hours afterwards before most of them recovered their usual quickness of hearing. The blast was very satisfactory: nothing remained but to clear away a few fragments, and the way to the steps lay open.

Rankler and the doctor went first; but just at the top of the steps they found their way blocked by a large rock, which, to their surprise, showed by its raw upper surface that it had just been detached from the wall. A glance was sufficient to detect the place from which it had fallen. It was quite easy to scramble over this block, but the explorers paused.

"This spells danger, Rankler. If the walls are in such a state, we may be entombed at any moment. This rotten limestone is in a very shaky state."

"I don't think there's any danger—at any rate, so long as we don't blast. Let's push on."

In a few minutes they were in the presence of the skeleton at the end of the passage. It was no longer sitting as Ned had described it; there was, in fact, nothing but a little heap of bones.

"That explosion of ours," shouted the doctor, "seems to have done a lot of damage: it has entirely disarticulated this skeleton."

"Look at this block," roared back Rankler, who had been examining the end of the passage. "This is no natural end to this gallery. There's been a tumble down at this end as well as at the other."

"Looks like it," was the reply. "But it isn't one block this time; there's a perfect heap of stones fallen along with it. What do you make of it all?"

"Same as you, I think. It must have been either an earthquake—or powder; and I daresay you agree with me in saying powder?"

"If we could only galvanize this chap into life for five minutes, we'd soon know all about it. But it's precious little he can tell us in his present state; yet, after all, he may tell us something."

As the doctor spoke he bent suddenly down, and showed a couple of bones sticking out from under the block that obstructed the passage.

"Poor fellow! his right leg was caught under this mass. What a death to die! Talk of a rat in a trap!"

"What sort of man would you say he was?" asked Rankler, taking up the breastplate that lay on the top of some of the bones, and from the arm-hole of which some scraps of what looked like leather still hung. "I mean, would you guess him to be a common soldier or a gentleman, or maybe a sailor—I suppose sailors wore this sort of thing long ago?"

The breastplate was so rusty that almost nothing could be made out of it. The headpiece, however, from its very shape seemed to suggest the sort of thing ordinary troopers wore at one time or another in English history. No spurs were found, which surprised Rankler, and confirmed the doctor in his view that the skeleton had belonged to a feudal Tommy Atkins. After examining the fingers in vain for rings, the doctor gave his opinion.

"A common soldier, I think, and a powerful fellow he must have been. I wish I knew more about the shapes of helmets at the different times. I suppose an antiquary could tell us to within a year or two when this tragedy occurred."

"In that case we are sure to get at the bottom of the affair sooner or later; but in the meantime I want to know what you think of the cause of this poor fellow's death—accident or design?"

"Accident, emphatically," replied the doctor; "walls don't fall to order."

"Then you agree with me that a big blast must have been made in the cave yonder, and that this falling in was the result?"

"It's all guess-work, of course, but it looks like that. We can't do better than go back and explore the cave itself. We may get some light under that heap of stones. It must have been there that the big explosion took place."

The blue-jackets were soon busily engaged at a kind of work that was very unusual to them. They were rather awkward with pick and shovel, to be sure; but they were very strong and willing, and the broken stones and rubbish soon began to pile up at the sides of the cave, leaving a great gap in the middle.

Meanwhile Rankler and the doctor were examining the remaining part of the staircase, and speculating as to how the structure had been originally completed. As it was, the remaining portion was merely hanging on nothing, there being no under support whatever. That only a part and not the whole had fallen at the explosion was a high compliment to the at least four-hundred-year-old workmanship. As Briggs ventured to remark, "Lime wasn't sand in th' old days."

"My opinion is that the staircase was deliberately blown up to cut off access from above," said Rankler.

"But in that case, how did—"

At this point a sailor came forward, as if in answer to the doctor's incomplete question, saluted Rankler, and presented, with a mixture of pride and horror, the ragged remains of the upper part of a skull.

"Hullo! where did you get this?"

Jack pointed with modest pride to the part of the *débris* at which he had been working.

When the doctor and Rankler had clambered up to the edge of the excavations, they found Martin and Wallace inside, apparently wrangling over something.

"It's an ancient pot, I tell you," Wallace maintained.

"An ancient grandmother," retorted Martin. "It's a bit of armour, as clear as daylight. It's been knocked about a good deal, I admit; and to tell the truth, I can't just say what bit it is, but it's a bit of armour, all the same."

The doctor supported Martin, and from that time onward there was more care exercised in digging, in case anything might be damaged that could supply a clue.

By this time all were quite convinced that an explosion had taken place. The fracture of the stones, and their very colour, seemed to prove it.

All this was very disappointing to Ned; for though everything appeared to prove the truth of the treasure story, everything seemed also to show that the treasure itself had gone up in smoke.

As they got deeper into the heap the explorers found the fragments of all kinds much smaller; indeed, "dust and ashes" pretty well describes what they found. But among this black stuff many queer things turned up, notably a large signet-ring. The broad band of gold was smashed almost flat, and would have been quite flattened had it not been for what looked like a small pebble that kept the two sides from meeting. After examining it for a few moments, the doctor horrified them all by explaining that this apparent pebble was really all that remained of a Tudor finger-bone.

The skull should have been much more horrible; but this little slice of finger-bone somehow got a bigger grip of their imaginations, and produced more shivers. Fortunately the stone on which the seal was engraved was not broken.

"More work for the antiquary," remarked Rankler, as he noted the crest.

"What antiquary?" asked Ned curiously.

"Oh, any antiquary. The doctor and I were talking about having an expert to examine all the antiquities we gather, and see what he can make of them."

"I know the very man," cried Ned, full of memories of Patterscriever's enthusiasm for old things, including maps. "The curator of the museum at Sardon is just steeped in knowledge like that."

"Maybe he'll be able to explain, then, what this is," cried Wallace, holding up an iron case that looked as if the upper part should come off as a sort of lid.

"This certainly promises well," remarked the doctor, shaking his head wisely; "but we must wait for information till the blacksmith interviews this box. The lid is almost welded into the rest, and we must be careful in forcing it open."

By this time the central part of the floor of the cave was pretty well cleared, and quite a collection of more or less interesting remains had been heaped up in a convenient corner near the steps that led into the gallery. Partly from the spurs—there were three of them in all, two of them obviously a pair—partly from the bones, they came to the conclusion that there had been two men engaged in this business; but after a more careful examination, the doctor saw reason to maintain that at least three men had been present. His reason was that three of a certain bone had been found, and it appears that each human being is supplied with only one of those bones. When questioned as to how this particular man happened to have none of the commoner bones, he answered that perhaps some of the bones in the heap did belong to this mysterious third party. But, besides, it was at least possible that one of the men had been nearer the explosion point than the others, and thus had been sent into smaller pieces. The others being placed at a little distance, may have been killed without being annihilated altogether, though, of course, they would be buried under the *débris.*

All this argument, however, came out at a later stage; on this first occasion there was room only for wonder at the traces of the awful explosion.

"What a blast it must have been!" exclaimed the doctor. "See how deep a hole it has torn in the solid rock."

As a matter of fact, there was a deep, ragged trench just under the spot where the staircase must have terminated when the vault was perfect.

"Strange that it should have ploughed so deep," said Rankler, who knew more about explosions and their effects, "when it had room to expand upwards. I take it that that hole was cut out *before* the explosion."

"Just look at the edges," began the doctor; but

added less confidently, "But, of course, they'd be torn up in any case."

It was Martin who first found a clue to the true state of affairs by jumping into the hole that had been cleared, and examining the edges a little bit lower than the level of the floor of the vault.

"This is not rock, but metal," he cried, as he ran his fingers along one of the sides.

"So it is," exclaimed Rankler: "things *are* getting complicated. It looks as if—"

Here Rankler stopped. Perhaps he was angry at what he saw; perhaps he was only struck dumb by surprise. One fact only was clear: *Martin had certainly winked.*

Now a naval officer is not accustomed to be winked at, so we need not be astonished at Rankler's amazement; but there is cause for astonishment at the result of that wink. It was not a common wink; it certainly was not a funny one. It was a sort of shorthand wink, which the lieutenant somehow seemed to be able to translate by a kind of instinct into a whole longhand speech.

"There's no good wasting any more time here," cried Martin, springing out of the hole and ostentatiously knocking the dust off his trousers.

Rankler, applying his translation of the wink, proceeded to get his men to pack up.

"But, I say, you're not going to give up yet," protested Ned, who had not seen, or at any rate had not been able to translate, the shorthand wink. But a dig in the ribs from Martin let him know that something was in the wind; so he accepted the situation like the rest, and went up with them to the open air. After lunching on the provisions brought from the ship, all the Weasels were sent back, except the sentinel and a petty officer and Briggs.

As soon as the men had gone, Rankler demanded,—

"Well, Mr. Martin, I see there's something important in the wind; what is it?"

"Well, sir, unless I've got jaundice and am seeing everything yellow, there's a lot of precious metal at the bottom of that iron hole."

"But surely my men are quite reliable; what need for all this secrecy?"

"There are enough of us as it is. They were only in the way, and I want Ned to find the stuff."

"Humph!" muttered Rankler; "I wonder if he has any real reason."

Leaving the two sailors at the entrance, the seven descended once more. Ned was sent first into the hole, and a very short examination showed that Martin's eyes had not deceived him. Ned had often wondered whether it would be gold vessels or gold money. As things turned out, it appeared to be neither. Whatever it had been before, it now appeared to be nothing but a shapeless mass of yellow metal. It formed a big lump like a huge nugget, for the explosion seemed to have welded it into a single mass.

"We've found the treasure, Ned," whispered Tony. "Now we must report it at once, in case there is any trouble."

"Time enough, Tony, when we get aloft." Then Ned turned to Rankler, and asked,—

"How much do you think it is worth, sir?"

"To tell the truth, I have not the faintest idea. I'm sure I never saw so much gold in my life—if it is gold."

This doubt at once produced a bottle that the doctor had brought for this very purpose. After a few minutes he stated quite confidently that the yellow stuff *was* gold.

Then they started trying to find out how deep the layer of gold was, but could make no progress at all. It seemed terribly wasteful to stand—actually to stand

—upon gold. No doubt it did not look particularly pretty, discoloured as it was on the surface, and mixed with sand and cinders. Yet while they knew that their picks would easily go through it, no one suggested the use of the pick.

In truth, the explorers found themselves face to face with the very serious problem of what was now to be done with the treasure.

"Wasn't I right in getting rid of your men without letting them know?" demanded Martin.

"Perhaps: but it seems to me we must send for some of them, all the same, in order to carry this thing off; or if not, at least to mount guard. We cannot leave this sort of thing lying about unprotected."

"How in all the world do they cut gold?" murmured the doctor discontentedly. He knew chemistry fairly well, but he had never had occasion to deal with this element in the lump before.

It was Rankler who suggested the cutting away of the soft rock round the iron chest, and then perhaps lifting out the whole thing. This was done so far as the cutting away of the rock was concerned, and that with almost no difficulty. The bottom of the chest was reached with comparative ease.

In fact, they were all disappointed at getting to the bottom so soon. They had hoped that the box would be deeper; indeed, they had hoped that it would not be a box at all, but an iron chamber.

Their hopes were clearly baffled, for it was obviously nothing but a very large iron chest, all the upper part of which was lacking, and all the bottom and sides of which had been twisted out of shape.

In the light of this limited capacity, the question of how much was again raised, but again received no very satisfactory answer.

"It may be worth anything between £10,000 and £1,000,000, for all that I know," was the doctor's confession.

Then there arose a contention about the size of the Welcome nugget. Opinions differed as much about that as about its value. The doctor had a vague idea that it was as big as a baby, and brought about £5,000. Tony did not know the size—that was not in his geography book at school—but he was positive about its value, for he remembered well getting up the pleasant fact that it brought its lucky finders the comfortable sum of £8,376, 10s. 6d.

"If we knew the weight we could tell," said the doctor: "every ounce is worth £3, 17s. 10½d."

"Hold on a minute, then," answered Tony, the arithmetician, fumbling in his pocket for his pencil. In a few minutes he had produced the result—that the nugget must have weighed at least 2,148 ounces troy weight, or 179 pounds.

"Let's have it in plain provision pounds," complained Martin, who was none too sure of the difference between troy and avoirdupois.

Tony was ready in a twinkling with another answer.

"One hundred and thirty-four and a quarter pounds avoirdupois gives £8,376, 10s. 6d."

"In plain English," said the doctor, after scribbling for a minute in his note-book, "a hundredweight of gold is worth very nearly £7,000."

"Is that all?" was Ned's disappointed exclamation. For, after all, £7,000 seems a small sum to a man who deals in gold by the hundredweight.

"You greedy little fellow!" replied the doctor. "I'm sure there's a ton of gold here, and that runs to £140,000 sterling, and you ask if that is all."

However, in the meantime nothing more definite could be made out, and there remained the practical difficulty of removing the treasure to a safe place. Tony was deputed to go to Sardon, and get some small but very strong packing-cases, into which the gold should be packed for transhipment to the *Weasel*. How the gold was to be cut into the requisite pieces was not yet discovered. But they had almost the whole afternoon before them to consult about it, while Tony started away at once to do his part of the work.

CHAPTER XV.

TONY'S EXPEDITION.

TONY was willing to be of service to his friends in any way they might desire, but he was not quite satisfied with this commission to get a supply of packing-cases. He felt that it made too small a demand on his intellectual powers. So he privately made up his mind to undertake and carry out a much more important and delicate mission for those he had left behind.

On reaching Sardon, however, he found that he had rather underestimated the difficulty of buying packing-cases, ready-made, of a particular size and strength. The packing-case makers that he called upon were all eager to undertake his order; and when they knew how pressed he was for time, they offered to supply the cases in a fabulously small number of hours, though their men would require to work all night, at time-and-a-half wages, to get the order completed.

When it was quite clear that he must have the cases that afternoon or not at all, the case-makers suggested various merchants in town who might possibly have something of the kind in their lumber-rooms.

It was a weary round through the grocers, the buttermen and cheesemongers, the drapers and haberdashers, with a look in at a certain coalman who was suggested as a possible dealer. It was in a bookseller's place that a set of fourteen cases were shown, which, being prepared to carry certain heavy books to local libraries, were provided with iron clasps along all the edges, and were made of sufficiently thick wood.

Unfortunately the bookseller was not only greedy but curious. Tony did not object to the exorbitant price, for he was well provided with money, and did not know the real value of his purchase. But he did object to being questioned as to the use the boxes were to be put to. It only whetted the man's curiosity when Tony said that they were merely to carry some things of value. Question followed question, till Tony began to despair of getting the boxes at all, so suspicious did the man become. Probably had the bookseller been only inquisitive and not also greedy, the bargain would not have been made.

But when he saw that the boy would not speak, he grumblingly concluded the transaction, and told Tony to come back at seven, when the boxes would be duly emptied of their present contents and handed over to him, if he came with a proper conveyance.

This delay was aggravating in some respects, but it had its compensations. It enabled Tony to carry out an idea he had in his mind. Walking along Westgate, the chief thoroughfare of Sardon, he examined the windows of one or two jewellers' shops, and finally selected the one that showed the most imposing array of gold articles. He asked to see some gold scarf-pins.

"Real gold, you know," he said, in his best off-hand way—"none of your electro-plate."

The well-dressed shopman looked queerly at this unlikely purchaser of real gold articles, but Tony's obviously marine flavour seemed to satisfy him. A sailor lad fresh from a long voyage is as promising a customer as a jeweller need wish for. Only sailor lads are not usually so particular about the quality of their gold.

Tony was soon busy in the midst of a blue plush pin-cushion filled with the cheapest nine carat gold scarf-pins. So far as size went, they were certainly excellent value for the money asked for them.

The shopman kept an exceedingly sharp eye on the lad, as he pulled out and critically examined each pin in turn; for shopmen get very clever at knowing how honest buyers behave, and how dishonest buyers differ from the genuine sort.

Tony, unfortunately, happened—though perfectly honest—to behave in the way common among dishonest customers, and thus roused the shopman's suspicions. It appears that your honest sailor lad or country bumpkin selects the biggest pin he can get for his money, places it against his breast, and tries to catch the effect in a mirror. You may have noticed that jewellers' shops have always lots of mirrors.

Tony, on the other hand, did not seem to care about personal effect at all; his interest was centred entirely in the pin, not in the more or less brilliant pebbles with which the head was ornamented.

"Real gold?" said Tony, looking up from one of the sturdiest pins in the cushion.

"Yes," was the dry reply.

"How do you know?"

"Don't you see the hall-mark?" asked the shopman, pointing to a little indentation at the back of the head of the pin.

Though he had exceedingly good eyes, Tony could make nothing out of the hall-mark, so he went on with his investigations.

"But if there weren't any hall-mark, how could you be sure it is gold?"

"All our things are hall-marked; but if need be, we can test gold with an acid that we keep."

"Oh," said Tony, not at all noticing how dry the shopman had become. In fact, the boy thought himself particularly wily in all this, leading up, as he was, to the next, which was the crucial point.

"Could you cut this pin in two?"

"Oh yes."

By this time the man was quite convinced that Tony was a swindler of some new kind. The very dullest shopman would have suspected him; for poor Tony had not even asked the price of the particularly thick pin he had selected. Still, as it was near closing time, and there was no other customer in the shop, the man thought he would humour the lad. It is a weary business keeping a shop where customers are rare. The man was glad of this opportunity of talking to some one. Besides, it is necessary for a good shopman to know all the new tricks. Accordingly the man replied mildly,—

"A file would do."

"But if you had a bigger bit of gold now, too big for a file, what would you do?"

"How big a lump of gold do you mean?"

"Oh, a big chunk—maybe the size of a—a—well, of a cheese. What would you do then?"

"Well, to tell you the truth, I'd want to know where you'd got it."

Too late, Tony saw that he had given himself away, and hastened to say that it was only from general interest he was asking.

"And you don't want a scarf-pin at all?"

This was asked in such an exceedingly disagreeable way, that Tony felt justified in playing the part of a good customer whom rudeness had driven from the shop. So he retorted, with as much dignity as the snub had left in him,—

"Well, no; you hardly seem to have anything quite good enough."

It was now getting dark, so Tony did not notice that the jeweller's boy followed him unostentatiously out of the shop, and kept him in sight for the next few minutes while he was on his way to the George, where he went to order a light van to convey his precious cases to the abbey.

As soon as the jeweller's boy found out that a van had been ordered, he felt that there was no longer any need to dog the steps of the suspicious character. He accordingly made direct for the police station, and said that his master had ordered him to report that a shady sham customer needed attention. To his surprise, he found that the police had already heard of the sailor lad through the bookseller, who had somehow got the idea that his boxes were being bought to help in some burglary. The two reports supported each other so well that it was determined to send a sergeant and a constable on the track of this suspicious character, on the principle that prevention is better than cure.

Tony was kept waiting at the bookseller's much longer than he had expected, but the bookseller was not to blame. It was the George people who were a little dilatory in sending the van. When it did arrive, Tony was greatly disgusted to find, instead of the light van he had ordered, one of those huge two-horse wagon affairs, with a rounded awning over it.

It was now too late to do anything to repair the blunder. Already he had delayed too long, and his friends at the abbey must by this time be uneasy. So Tony ordered the man to bundle in the cases and start at as good a pace as such an old traction-engine of an affair could be expected to keep up.

"The two horses'll cost twice as much as I intended; but, after all, that doesn't matter—treasure-finders can't grudge trifles like these."

But he might have really grudged the extra charge if he had had the remotest idea that it included the fares of a fat sergeant and a lean constable, who were safely tucked away at the back of the wagon.

When at last they came near their destination, Tony told the man that he needn't drive round to the gate of the abbey. If he laid the boxes against the abbey wall at the corner of the Sardon Road and the shore lane, they would be picked up the first thing in the morning. Nobody would touch them, and old Mr. Brownjohn did not allow wagons to enter the gate after dark.

"All right," said the driver; and the two free passengers chuckled, and felt glad they had come. It was not to be a wild-goose chase after all.

While the boxes were being piled up, the two policemen got softly out, and sheltered themselves behind the trees on the opposite side of the road.

The wagon drove off, and as soon as it was fairly out of hearing, Tony gave the whistle that had been agreed upon. It was at once answered.

"I 'ope 'tain't poachin'," groaned the fat one.

Catching poachers, you will understand, is a dangerous game, and not at all included in the ordinary duties of a Sardon policeman.

"But wot 'ud poachers want wi' cuttin' gold?" answered the lean one, somewhat to the comfort of his chief. After all, burglars are not necessarily provided with firearms.

By-and-by a sound was heard on the other side of the wall, then the clinking of iron on the top, and soon Ned's head appeared. The ladder was drawn up from the inside and let down on the outside.

A gruff voice from beyond the wall gave some advice to Ned.

"There's three on 'em," groaned the fat one.

"An' there's another," grumbled the lean one, as Wallace's voice was heard talking to Briggs, who was responsible for the gruff voice.

"Let's seize them young fellers afore t'others come over," whispered the fat one.

"Let's bolt," murmured the lean one.

In tremulous whispers they discussed the situation.

When Ned had got fairly down, they had an opportunity of gauging his fighting powers, and as a consequence came to quite a gallant decision. They would rush out, seize the two lads, catch the ladder and unhook it before the others could come over to the rescue, and then they would hurry off their prisoners to the wagon, which was waiting for them, by arrangement, a little bit down the road.

At least the first part of this programme was carried out. In the charge Ned fell to the lot of the lean one, who made a very successful thing of it; for our friend was on his face in the grass in no time, and the lean one's knee was pressed with uncomfortable emphasis between his shoulders.

The fat one was not so happy. Either he was slower than his lean friend, or Tony was quicker than Ned, for in this case the charge met a prepared foe. Of course it is very wrong to hit below the belt, but with a man three times your own weight it may be permitted, particularly if he happens to be a policeman. These were the principles on which Tony acted, at any rate, and by the time the fat one had recovered sufficiently to sit up, it was to see his opponent squatting on the top of the wall.

No doubt you are surprised to find him there.

You expected to hear of him on the top of the lean one, who was on the top of Ned. But Tony knew a trick worth two of that. The rope-ladder was up like winking, and down on the other side; and before the fat one had quite recovered himself, and before the lean one had quite driven the last breath out of Ned, Wallace and Briggs were on the scene.

The coastguardsman lifted the lean one by the coat collar and the seat of his trousers from his dangerous work on Ned. Then explanations began.

For finding himself still alive, though he had some difficulty in believing it, the sergeant demanded what mischief they had been up to. The words were bold, and in face of such odds sounded not badly, but there was an unexpectant ring about them. He spoke for the honour of his uniform, nothing more. The lean one held his peace.

For reply, Briggs turned the sergeant's own bull's-eye upon the official cap that showed his connection with the preventive service.

"Oh—ah! that's a different matter. Why didn't you tell us that at first? then there'd been no 'arm done."

Tony pointed out sarcastically that the time devoted to introductions before the scrimmage had been quite insufficient for full explanations, and concluded by asking what the policemen wanted there anyway, and how they got there.

"We came i' the wagon along o' you," stated the lean one, thinking he was doing his superior a service; whereas that ill-used person was holding his tongue only because he was too slow-witted to invent a more creditable explanation than the shameful truth.

"And what brought you sneaking here?" roared Tony, trying to hide in dramatic indignation the shame he felt at having been so easily hoodwinked as to bring his own captors with him.

"Well, we 'ad information agin you from two shopkeepers," answered the sergeant, with an aggrieved air. "There was Sinnesheim and Co., an'—"

"Who's Sinnesheim and Co.?" demanded Wallace; "and what had they to do with it?"

"They're the jewellers in Westgate. An' the report we got was—"

"Clay up!"

This, I regret to say, was Tony's vulgar way of asking the fat one to hold his peace. But something may be pardoned in a boy driven to despair by the fear of an exposure of his unsuccessful efforts to discover the best way of cutting gold.

The sergeant "clayed up," for he also had no great reason to be proud of his night's work. He was glad of an excuse to cut short his shameful story. Yet he did not like the idea of going away with his tail quite between his legs, if for no other consideration than the loss of dignity it implied in the eyes of his lean follower.

"You will, of course, give me your names and addresses," he said, with all the swagger he had left. "I mean your real names and addresses."

"Archie Campbell, Berth 37CA, Broomielaw, Glasgow," replied Tony, giving the nearest approach to a true answer that he could hit upon.

It was not till this had been written down—with the help of Tony, who generously gave the sergeant a lift over the stony places of the spelling—that the policeman realized how useless it was.

"But, I say, this ain't no good. W'ere did you sleep last night?"

"On board H.M.S. *Weasel*," replied Tony, with emphasis.

This concluded the case so far as the fat one was concerned. He felt that a hornet's nest was much nearer the truth than even a mare's nest in describing his present position; so he politely wished the four good-night, and led his man off to the not very distant wagon. Officer and man were alike overjoyed to go, though both had a moment or two's anxiety, in their first step of retreat, lest an attack should be made on their rear.

While the two outraged policemen were being driven back to Sardon in sullen silence, the treasure-seekers merrily tossed over the fourteen cases that Tony had brought. Fourteen does not divide neatly by four, so Tony had to carry the rope-ladder to make up for having only two cases to carry.

As they approached the cave Briggs explained that the investigations had proceeded during Tony's absence, and that they had at last fallen back upon a plain axe to cut up the gold. It was felt that, after all, this would do no harm to the gold, which would have to be melted again in any case. Besides, there would be no sparks of gold lost, as it was not brittle.

As they had got down a little bit in the chest, however, it was found that the mass was not solid, as they had supposed.

"You don't mean to say the bottom was empty?" demanded Tony suspiciously, wondering if there had been some deep-laid plan in getting him out of the way in order to get the better of trustful Ned.

"Not quite empty," returned Ned; "but the bottom of the chest was filled with gold vessels and things like that."

"Empty gold jugs!" sniffed Tony disgustedly; "why, that'll reduce the value to a quarter of what we thought."

"Well, not quite," replied Ned cheerily; "for some of the things are half covered with precious stones, so that maybe they are worth far more than three or four times their weight in gold."

"How do you know they're precious stones?"

"Oh, well, as to that we're not quite sure, you know. But they all think they are precious stones; and what would those old fellows do putting bits of coloured glass on real gold vessels and mitres?"

"Maybe you're right; I hope so anyway," was the only reply that could be drawn from the gloomy Tony.

While waiting for the cases, the others had made a collection of suitable packing in the form of dry rushes and grasses, so that when Tony did arrive it was not long before everything was ready to transport the treasure on board.

There was found to be quite enough room in the fourteen cases, and somewhat to the disappointment of everybody, though no one said a word about it, the boxes could be carried about with the greatest ease. None of them exceeded a hundredweight, and most of them fell a good deal below that.

Before midnight the whole of the cases were aboard the *Weasel*, and nothing but an unattractive array of carefully-assorted bones could tempt any one to invade the cave.

The Campadder treasure was at length secured.

CHAPTER XVI.

THE STRUGGLE WITH BOX NO. 4.

HAPPY as Ned and his friends were at their find, the happiness of Mr. Patterscriever was quite as great when he was summoned to the *Weasel*, and had the various odds and ends submitted to him for his opinion upon them.

About the breastplate and headpiece found in the gallery he was quite clear. They certainly belonged to the period of Edward the Sixth or Mary, and they belonged as certainly to a common soldier. They were good and serviceable of their kind, but that kind was common.

The crest on the ring he did not at once recognize. He would require time to look up his books to make sure to which family it belonged—if, indeed, it belonged to any English family; of which he was doubtful, for he thought he knew the crests of all the local gentry for the past century or two.

The iron case, however, promised more definite information. Thanks to the skill of the engineer, the cover was detached from the case without any damage to the contents, which in their turn were carefully extracted. They proved to be two documents carefully folded. One was large and important-looking; the other was small and apparently insignificant.

It was the insignificant paper that attracted the greater attention. For though the big paper had a magnificent seal hanging to it, it was written in Latin, and old-fashioned Latin at that. None of the explorers could make anything of it, so it was at once handed over to Patterscriever; while the rest gave all their attention to the small paper, on which was very roughly drawn a sort of map or picture.

There was first a discussion as to which was the right end up. The position of the ship made one end the top; the position of the figures made the other. Patterscriever set this matter right by explaining that in old drawings like this both ends were top, according as the draughtsman turned the map this way or that. The antiquary, however, soon turned his attention entirely to his Latin document, and left the others to puzzle out the drawing.

It was Tony who first suggested the true explanation, by asking what those queer things *like stairs* could mean.

"You've hit it, my lad," cried Rankler: "stairs they are, and the whole thing is a chart of the treasure-cave."

The others looked a little incredulous, and Wallace wanted to know what the little wheel in the centre could mean, in that case.

"Why, don't you see, that's the very thing that makes me sure it's the cave. That stands for the staircase that has been blown up."

"Then what are those squares with the numbers?" asked Tony, with excitement fairly well kept under.

"I can't say," replied Rankler slowly, looking steadily at Tony the while. "Have you any theory?"

"It strikes me they're treasure-chests, and we've only got one."

"And we've left the whole place open," moaned Ned.

"Why, my lad, not a soul except ourselves knows that any treasure has been found, though I daresay some of our fellows have an inkling of the value of the cases they had a hand in carrying aboard last night."

"Which of the four do you think we have unearthed?" asked Martin, trying to get his bearings among the four squares.

"No. 3, I should say,'" replied Rankler. "I hope they go in ascending order. No. 4 should be worth something handsome."

While they talked quietly enough, there was an under-current of excitement. As it was, their find was magnificent, but this scrap of paper seemed to hold out hopes of quadruple gain.

It was agreed that none of the men should be taken on this new expedition. There were eight of themselves as it was, including the antiquarian, whom they thought it desirable to have with them.

Arrived at the cave, they saw cause to regret having no able-bodied sailors to help in the work of clearing away the rubbish; for they could not get at No. 1 because of the rubbish that had been heaped in that quarter. They all took a turn, however, except the doctor, and, of course, Patterscriever. As soon as the floor was cleared at the desired place, certain seams became plain, and indicated the possibility of a stone lid.

In spite of the best efforts of the explorers, the stone lid would not yield. It was necessary to break through by means of the pick. The work took but little time. In a few minutes Briggs' pick went right through the soft stone, to his surprise, and to the uneasiness of the rest.

Soon the melancholy truth became clear. There was the stone receptacle right enough, but the iron chest that they had been confident it would contain was not there. Nothing but an empty hole rewarded all their efforts. The hole seemed in every respect like that containing the treasure; it differed only in being empty.

"Could it have been emptied since we were here?" asked Tony doubtfully. But the appearance of the whole thing, inside and out, loudly proclaimed that nineteenth-century interference had had nothing to do with the barrenness of the hole.

It was now the turn of No. 2. With less hope but more energy the explorers cleared the way to it, and smashed in the top as before. As before, the thing was empty.

"Is it worth trying the No. 4?" asked Ned, disconsolately gazing into the empty gulf of No. 2.

Briggs' reply was a sturdy whack with his pick in the required direction. Up to a certain point their experience with this opening was the same as it had been with the others. The picks finally, as before, found their way through the stone covering; this stone at last gave way and fell in. It was here that the difference began. The fragments of the covering did not fall quite to the bottom. As soon as the rubbish was removed, an iron chest was exposed.

It was not nearly so large as the remains of the first chest, which was disappointing; it had nothing like the same weight, which was more so. Briggs and Wallace easily managed between them to hoist up the box. The coastguardsman, indeed, maintained that he could have lifted the whole affair himself.

"Not much treasure this journey," condoled Wallace; then added as a happy after-thought, "Unless this thing's filled wi' bank-notes."

"Bank-notes in 1554!" groaned Tony.

At an earlier stage of his life Wallace would here have blushed at his own ignorance, but now experience had taught him never to blush before his juniors. He contented himself with saying,—

"Had me there, Tony. But let's see what *is* in it. I only hope it's not empty like the holes."

"A queer lock this," cried Rankler, who had been kneeling examining the box. "It seems fairly sturdy. How are we to get in?"

"Oh, we can't stop to pick a Tudor lock," said Martin; "we must smash it in. It's a pity it wasn't open like the other.—Hand over your hammer and chisel, Briggs."

"Hold on," commanded Rankler, in his official tones; then added more gently, "Don't let's do anything rash. There's something queer about the blow-up at the other box. How was none of the gold blown out of the box when the stairs were blown up?"

"Because the gold was blown down, of course," answered Martin. "That seems clear enough. The explosion smashed all the top vessels into a solid lump, leaving only the bottom vessels as they were."

"As clear as day," assented Rankler, a little absently; "but maybe you do not quite see the force of my argument. Your belief is that since the explosion took place above, it must have blown the metal down?"

"Of course." This with a very surprised look.

"Now, would you call iron a metal?"

"Of course. Eh—you don't mean—"

"I mean that I want you to tell me what became of the lid of that chest. If the explosion took place at the foot of the stair, the lid would certainly have suffered, but it would have been blown down. No doubt it would have been blown out of all shape, but there would have been some iron left among the gold."

"In plain English what's your opinion?" asked Martin uneasily. "I hate guessing about things like this."

"But mine is, after all, only a guess; I give it for what it is worth. You've all heard about old-fashioned treasure-chests. Now it used to be not uncommon to protect such chests by a clockwork arrangement connected with the lock, which exploded a mixture to the serious damage of any one who did not know the proper way to open the chest."

"So you think those fellows"—here Martin pointed to the assorted bones in the corner—"were poachers on this preserve who knew nothing about the lock of the treasure-box, and so brought the stair down about their ears?"

"Well, that's about it. But, of course, it's only a guess, and may be all wrong."

The highest compliment to Rankler's theory was paid by the unanimity with which everybody quitted the neighbourhood of the newly-unearthed box.

"What's to be done now?" asked Martin, indignantly eyeing the disturbing box.

"Wouldn't it be safer in its hole again?" suggested

Tony. "If it goes off there, it will all go straight up, and not hurt any of us."

"Right y'are, my boy. You just chuck it in again, will ye?"

It was Briggs who spoke; but Tony had his retort ready.

"You were bragging a minute ago that you could lift it yourself. Now's your time."

To tell the truth, Wallace and Briggs were feeling streams of cold water running down their backs, as they thought of the horrible danger they had just run in tossing about this infernal machine.

"Seems to me," said Rankler, "that the best thing we can do now is to blow up the thing ourselves, before it has time to blow us up."

"But wouldn't that waste a lot of treasure?" asked Ned anxiously.

"You greedy fellow, aren't you content with the enormous haul you have made? If you're so anxious for more, take Briggs' hammer and chisel and smash open the lid."

Without a word Ned seized the tools and made for the box. Briggs made at once for the gallery. Martin and Wallace fell into each other's arms in the No. 1 hole. Tony disappeared behind the heap of rubbish near the wall. Even Patterscriever seemed to realize that something required to be done in self-defence; but before he could make up his mind on the point the danger was past, for Rankler had seized Ned's shoulder, and cried,—

"You've got grit as well as greed, my lad. But we mustn't let you throw your life away—not to speak of our own."

As the others began to emerge from their hiding-places, Mr. Patterscriever remarked,—

"I have been trying to remember the exact date at which the locksmith's art was first applied to purposes of defence in the matter of treasure-chests. I know it was at Nürnberg it began, but I cannot for the life of me recollect when. Besides, the art may have been practised in secret long before the honest Germans got hold of it."

As this left matters precisely where they were, Martin made a practical suggestion.

"Wouldn't it be a good idea to get a musket and take pot shots with ball cartridge at the lock? If the lock is up to any mischief, that would set it off."

"And what better would we be than if we had tackled it with the hammer and chisel?"

"We would be this the better, that being a sitting

shot we could aim the gun, get it fixed in position, and then pull the trigger by a string from a safe distance."

"From what we have seen, there appears to be no place safe within this cave while explosions are going on. The crumbling rock may anywhere come tumbling down about our ears."

Already they were getting familiar with this terrible box that had not yet gone off, and though this familiarity did not quite degenerate into contempt, it led to a less timid policy. It was agreed to carefully cord the box, and then have it fastened by two stout cords to a block-and-tackle arrangement on the surface.

They did not hope to be able in this way to drag the box to the top of the stairs—there were too many angles and turnings for that—but they thought that from the very number of obstacles they would be able to give the box such a thorough shaking up and such a bumping as would encourage it to do its worst down below there, where there was no one by to be injured.

Without very much trouble things were arranged so that the box was drawn up with great violence against the lowest step of the broken staircase, and bumped viciously against it. The sound of the concussion was clearly heard from above, but was followed by nothing more serious.

Next the rope was let run, and the box crashed down upon the floor of the cave. Still no remarkable result.

This was repeated several times with impunity, and at length, after the explorers had done their worst in ill-using the box, they determined to take the bull by the horns, and bring the suspected chest to the surface. Of the five volunteers for this duty Rankler selected Briggs and Martin.

This time the block and tackle were worked with all gentleness, and by their aid and the manual labour of Briggs and Martin the box was duly deposited on one of the flat paving-stones of the old abbey floor.

One could almost believe that the old box was blinking in the sunshine after all those years of dark imprisonment. It had suffered a little from its recent bad treatment, but really nothing to speak of. In fact, the knocks it had received appeared to have done nothing worse than expose various bits of raw metal that flashed defiantly in the sun.

The others sat down to lunch at a considerable distance from the uncanny box, but Briggs and Tony went off for a musket and ammunition. For while the severe handling the box had withstood proved that it could be dealt with as a whole without any special danger, it still remained to be seen whether an attempt on the lock would produce any formidable result.

It was somewhat peculiar gun practice. Rankler rather prided himself on his marksmanship, so the rifle was given to him. A range of one hundred and fifty yards was selected, and a cover of stones was arranged with quite a respectable sight-hole.

The first shot hit the copper facings of the key quite fairly, and nothing happened. Above and below and around the keyhole all bore marks of Rankler's skill before the explorers left their cover and approached, somewhat contemptuously, their target.

"I remember reading," began Mr. Patterscriever, "of an old chest of this kind that had a spring that let out a whole row of knives as soon as the lid was raised. It opened just like the jaws of a wild beast, and made a snap at any one whose head was within reach."

"'Old 'ard," growled Briggs, whose head was appointed to be nearest the opening chest, "or you'll gi' me the creeps."

"But," interposed Rankler, "you do not think that, after all, there may be some trick of an explosion with the lock?"

"Well, no," answered the old man thoughtfully; "I can only think of one danger now till the box is actually opened."

"Let's have it, by all means," cried Martin; "out with the last croak."

"I believe," went on Patterscriever, disregarding the young man's rudeness, "they sometimes arranged that if any but the right person opened the box, a whiff of poisonous gas should escape with fatal effect.—I believe, doctor, you'll admit that, whatever else they understood, they knew something about poisons in those old days, particularly in Italy; and I don't think Spain would likely be behind them, and this is obviously a Spanish box."

Nobody thought of asking how he knew that it was a Spanish chest; their interest was entirely taken up with this new suggestion of danger. It was with very great satisfaction that they heard the doctor's reply,—

"As to that, I don't think there can be much danger after all those years. However well sealed a gas may be, it must have—well, no, it may be kept in a hermetically-sealed glass; but still in the open air here, and—well, maybe the man who opens it should keep his mouth pretty tight just at first, and maybe he should wear gloves as well, in case of some nasty acid dodge."

Ned was eager to manipulate the chisel, but Briggs would have none of it. It is true that Briggs ran greater danger from acids, for he happened to be beyond sizes in gloves. He was prepared, however, to let his big hands take their chance, and in his own mind he had given up all feelings of respect for that paltry box. A box that had had such provocation as this one would have kicked long ago if there had been any kick in it.

At the first stroke of the hammer on the chisel that had been placed at the seam along the top there arose a little cloud of white dust. This would have raised no remark in ordinary circumstances, but now it made Briggs reconsider his contemptuous opinion of this spiritless box, and spring back to a respectful distance. Gunpowder was a thing Briggs could understand; poison was a different affair.

A moment's consideration showed that the white puff was nothing but the white dust which the box had gathered in its recent rough usage. Accordingly Briggs returned to the attack, and with somewhat unnecessary violence tore open the unwilling lid.

The contents were covered by a white cloth—at least it had been white. Ned tore it off eagerly, and was disappointed to find beneath nothing but a great heap of yellow papers.

"Maybe there's something below the beastly rubbish," growled Ned, as he plunged his hands under the papers at the sides of the box, and spilled some of them on the flags, to the intense disgust of Patterscriever, who gathered them up tenderly, with the protest,—

"Gold, forsooth! there's treasure here that no gold can buy."

Ned soon convinced himself and the others that the box contained nothing but the papers, so he discontentedly turned to Patterscriever to ask what they were all about anyway.

It appeared as if Nemesis had all too quickly overtaken the unsympathetic old antiquarian. It was now his turn to be disappointed, for sheet after sheet that he examined proved to be totally blank. Some of them appeared to have a few strange characters at the right hand bottom corner; but these marks he could not decipher, and most of the sheets had not even those meaningless marks.

"Not a word," complained Patterscriever, as he laid

down the last roll that he had hurriedly examined. "But, of course, it's far from hopeless. It goes without saying that they are all covered with invisible ink. No doubt that's why there was no guard on the lock. They depended on the sympathetic ink to hide their secrets from any one who chanced to hit upon the chest."

If Patterscriever was right in his guess, those old invisible-ink writers were justified in their confidence. Their secret was secure from all prying eyes for all time. Neither then nor later did any one make anything of the mysterious rolls.

Patterscriever was not to be blamed; it was certainly not for lack of effort on his part. He tried every reagent he knew of to coax back the old ink, but in vain. He steeped the papers in cold solutions, he steeped them in warm. He roasted them before his study fire; he all but boiled one in a copper-lined saucepan. But not a single character would appear.

Disappointed as the explorers were at the result of his investigations, they could not avoid a laugh occasionally at his comical despair. It was well that all his material did not turn out equally obdurate, or the poor man would have lost his head altogether.

As a matter of fact, he had made a great deal out of the big paper with the fat seal; but of what he had discovered he refused to utter a single syllable till he had consulted with Uncle Roland, whom he had specially sent for, and who was already on his way to Sardon.

CHAPTER XVII.

LAW AND JUSTICE.

"MR. CAMPADDER," began the antiquarian, as soon as he had met Uncle Roland at his rooms in the George at Sardon, "you will, I am sure, excuse the liberty I have taken in summoning a busy man like you. But the fact is that a paper has been discovered of such importance to your family that I have made a point of telling no one whatever of its contents before consulting you."

Uncle Roland cautiously acknowledged this kind consideration, and encouraged Mr. Patterscriever to go on with his story.

"The paper which I hold in my hand," went on the antiquarian, somewhat pompously, as he held up the larger of the two papers found in the iron case, "is a royal warrant granting the abbey and lands of Arnwyke, forfeited by the deceased Walter Campadder, to Hugh Fitzashby, Her Majesty's well-beloved, etc."

"What's the date of that precious document?"

"Fifteen hundred and fifty-six; and your title dates from 1537."

"Show me the deed."

Mr. Patterscriever handed over the well-preserved old parchment with its handsome seal almost intact; for the case had preserved it from anything but a severe pressure, which had somewhat spoiled the clearness of the lines, but nothing more.

Uncle Roland twisted the curious document up and down without very well knowing what he was doing, gaped at the seal, then, holding the parchment behind him, turned his back to the fire, and said, very deliberately,—

"Do you think there is any real danger to our former title in this rigmarole?"

"I cannot really say. That is a matter rather for modern lawyers, and isn't at all in my line. But I should suppose it would at least lead to complications."

"What's to hinder me from dropping it quietly into the fire as I stand?"

"Mr. Campadder! A perfect sixteenth-century document, *with* the seal!"

"You tell me you haven't shown it to any one;

so there can be no harm done by quietly disposing of it."

"At least you'll keep the seal for me; *it* can do your title no harm."

"So you do not think there is any moral wrong in destroying this paper? It has only a museum interest for you?"

"I was not thinking of the moral question at all. But so far as I can see, you need not be afraid of the Fitzashbys. I have looked up the records, and find that they died out just about the time this grant was made. It appears that Hugo—that is, this Hugo—and his son, his only child, sailed for the Spanish Main in the later years of Mary's reign, and were never heard of again."

"Till this week, eh?"

"Well, yes; I'm inclined to think so. The ring has the Fitzashby crest."

"What ring?"

Patterscriever explained, and gave it as his opinion that the Fitzashby family tree had been suddenly cut down in the vaults of Arnwyke Abbey.

"But if the abbey belonged to them, as this paper seems to show it did, why did they enter the vaults secretly, as they seem to have done, instead of boldly turning out the ruling Campadder, and searching the vaults at their leisure?"

"As to that I can say nothing; all I can say is that the ring, that paper, and the story of the disappearance of the two Fitzashbys, all fit into the theory that two of the skeletons—or, at any rate, one of the skeletons—belonged to the Fitzashbys."

"Since the Fitzashbys have been extinct more than three hundred and thirty years, I daresay I may treat this as waste paper. I suppose you do not happen to know if they have left any heirs-at-law traceable so far back?"

"I cannot at this moment say."

"Not that that matters much, for their claims must have long ago died out by what the lawyers call *prescription*."

"But if Sir Walter forfeited the lands by treason, would they not revert to the state, failing any legal heir of the Fitzashbys?"

"Oh, the prescription would apply to the crown's claim as well as to the others," said Uncle Roland uneasily, twirling about the dangerous paper, and trying to be as confident as his words.

"I should think so," said Patterscriever, with a confidence borrowed from the other. Besides, the more confidence, the better chance of saving the precious document from the flames.

"My best plan is to take this affair to Mr. Sarginiss, and get his opinion of the whole matter. I return to town to-morrow, at any rate, and I shall abide by his decision."

Mr. Patterscriever watched, with ill-concealed regret, the disappearance of the deed and seal into Uncle Roland's inside pocket. This subject was treated as closed, and the talk drifted into other channels. Speaking of the box of blank papers, Uncle Roland remarked,—

"I don't know that I am particularly anxious that you should succeed in deciphering them. Your catch in manuscript up till now does not encourage me to long for more."

"It may be that the blank papers will explain the whole thing, and I should not wonder if they entirely revolutionize our present ideas of the Tudor period. What would not Froude give for that boxful!"

"Not much in their present state, I daresay, but, of course, you may be able to make them tell their tale. But in any case you'll let me know their contents before you make them public, eh?"

The final word was uttered with unusual sharpness

for the antiquarian had suddenly put on a very constrained expression.

"Well, yes. But, you see, it has just occurred to me that in the meantime—I trust you will pardon me for pointing this out—the papers are not—well, not quite your property, and I'm, now that I think of it, particularly glad you did not destroy that parchment in your pocket."

"To whom do they belong, then? Ned is not of age."

"No. But—well, the treasure itself is in the meantime in the hands of the crown, and the parchment was handed to me by Lieutenant Rankler, whom I must regard as a representative of the crown. And he, of course, knows about the parchment, and it might be awkward for—well, for *you*—if it did not turn up when wanted."

Uncle Roland glared at the nervous speaker, but had too much wisdom to oppose a view that had so much common-sense to recommend it. His consolation was that, even if Arnwyke were taken from him, he would have to repay to Brownjohn only the original price, so that the worst loser would be that unamiable pottery man.

While Mr. Sarginiss was examining the paper next

day, our explorers were examining the gallery leading from the cave.

What puzzled them all was the absence of the gulf that the drawing showed at the end of the gallery. Everything else seemed so accurate that this difference from fact was incomprehensible. With one of the *Weasel's* boats they examined the coast carefully where the gulf was represented to be, but could make nothing of it different from the ordinary government charts.

Next they tried from the inside. Examination proved the truth of what they had only guessed— that the block of the gallery had occurred at the point where the angle was shown in the drawing. A little blasting was necessary to get the rubbish removed, and from previous experience they avoided the mistake of using too much powder.

Following the now open way, they soon came to a flight of rough steps cut out of the soft rock, and leading down to what was obviously water.

Not still water like that of a pond or ditch, but fresh and wholesome water that plashed about in a way that nothing short of a direct connection with the sea could explain. The weeds clinging to the steps, and to the walls so far as they could examine them, left the matter no longer in doubt. They were in presence of a large sheet of water cut off from, yet somehow connected with, the sea.

The water-cave was so large that their lights could not at all reach across it, nor indeed very far on either side of the steps on which they stood.

It required a good deal of preparation before a tiny boat could be conveyed down the winding stair into the treasure-cave and then along the gallery to the water-cave. But when it was once launched, the cave was carefully examined, and as a result the explorers came to the conclusion that this cave had been originally an open gulf, and that the rocks at the sides had, for some reason unknown, fallen in, and made it into the cave it now was.

This was the doctor's theory, though Rankler tried to hint at the possibility of its being built over to form a sort of hiding-hole for smuggling purposes.

"A much smaller affair would do for smuggling," argued the doctor. "And had I been a smuggler building a hole, I think I would have left an entrance."

The tide was clearly marked in the cave, and by careful soundings it was made out that about six fathoms below low-water mark there was a channel of some kind connecting the inner with the outer water. How wide the channel was could not be determined, and indeed by this time the interest of the explorers had greatly diminished. No fresh treasure had been discovered, nor the slightest hint of any. Accordingly all the interest centred in the distribution of what had actually been found.

The exact value of the treasure was never known, for the government officials rightly enough determined not to sell any of the fairly well preserved ecclesiastical vessels and ornaments. Many of them can be seen now in various museums throughout the country, and some of them, I believe, have been restored to certain of the cathedrals that could show some sort of claim to inherit them. Of those details I cannot speak with any certainty; but I have no doubt the government officials did what was right and just to all parties having reasonable claims.

At any rate, our friends had no cause to complain. By some mysterious arithmetical process, somebody in some government office came to the conclusion that Ned was entitled to something over £120,000. Ned did not turn to the end of the book to see whether the government man's answer was correct; he accepted it at once, and was glad.

The same government official had other sums to work and other answers to get; but none of our friends challenged his accuracy. They all got so much money that their main difficulty was to know what to do with it.

The only thing that Tony, for example, could think of doing with part of his £500 was to buy himself off from the *Arica*, and start fair under an easier skipper than Captain Fleming. But when he heard, to his great astonishment, that Ned was going to stick to the *Arica* till his apprenticeship was finished, he too made up his mind to hold on.

I daresay you will guess that Uncle Roland had something to do with Ned's resolution to finish his apprenticeship.

"A couple of years more in the tar-bucket," the old gentleman had said, "will make a man of you." And Ned had not been unwilling to be made a man of.

On the other hand, Uncle Roland took care that Mr. Griffins was continued on board the *Arica* till Ned's education (and Tony's) was completed; and that officer did not have any cause to regret his delayed promotion, either in the matter of pay or prospects.

At first it looked as if Ned too would not know what to do with his money, but Uncle Roland's communications with Mr. Sarginiss opened a way.

The lawyer pointed out that since the Fitzashbys had never really entered into possession, their claim was at least doubtful, and could be practically neglected, but that the estate might be resumed by the crown under some obscure old Act coupled with quite a recent enactment regarding inheritance.

Mr. Sarginiss wrote all this to Mr. Brownjohn, and at the same time found out, from important legal friends in the confidence of the government officials, that there was no intention on the part of the crown to make any claim.

This uncertainty annoyed Mr. Brownjohn a great deal, and was carefully increased by Mr. Sarginiss, with the result that before the *Arica* sailed Ned had the satisfaction of knowing that he was the possessor of Arnwyke Abbey and lands. At all events he was the practical possessor, though certain formalities had to be gone through after he had sailed. It is true that Brownjohn made something of the bargain after all, for the price Ned paid was one and a half what the old pottery man had paid to Uncle Roland. Even at this high price, however, the estate was an excellent bargain.

As you may believe, Ned did not spend all his holiday in knocking about among lawyers. There were certain people he wanted to see, notably the real Tony, about whom the reader may chance to be a little curious. Perhaps it has been hardly fair to let the new Tony so completely usurp the place of the old; but the truth is that the true Tony had led a very uneventful life during Ned's voyage. Mr. Darvel had persuaded Mrs. Wedgeworth to keep the boy absolutely limited to his shilling a week of pocket-money, and this comparative poverty had been very good for him. He had played much and worked a little, and the letters that Ned received from him became less picturesque as to the handwriting and less original as to the spelling.

From Sardon Ned wrote to Tony saying that he intended to run down to Merliston to see all his old friends; but when Tony had shown the letter to the head-master, that wily old gentleman suggested that it would be better for Tony to go to visit Ned. To tell the truth, it *is* wiser to give one boy a week's holiday than to permit a successful treasure-seeker to upset a whole school by his disturbing presence.

And thus it came about that the real Tony and the false met as Ned's guests.

From this time forward, however, Archie Campbell resumed his real name, though it involved the indignation of Captain Fleming, who strongly protested against such unsettling practices.

Another of Ned's guests at Sardon was even more interesting, being none other than our friend Old Hookey. Leave had been graciously granted to the old mariner to spend a week away from the ship, which was due to sail as soon as this week was up. The first three days of the leave were spent rather pleasantly by Hookey, who appeared to take very kindly to life at a small seaside inn, and Mrs. Peterson seemed to understand and appreciate all his little ways. Then, too, he had the interesting work of investigating the cave and the gallery and all the rest, and listened with great gravity to all everybody had to say. He even went the length of asking very many unconnected questions that nobody could guess the meaning of, but he never by any chance ventured on a suggestion of his own. Mr. Patterscriever, in particular, had cause to groan under the merciless cross-examination of the old salt; and when it was intimated that Uncle Roland had acceded to

Ned's urgent request, and had invited Old Hookey, along with the other Aricas, to stay the rest of his leave in the shipowner's grand house in London, nobody was more pleased than the worn-out antiquarian.

Certainly Old Hookey did not seem to value the honour at its true worth. He went to the grand house, it is true; but he soon regretted it.

It was not that he was overawed at the grandeur with which he was surrounded; he was simply bored by the senseless way people went on. Particularly he could not bear the silliness of the eternal hand-washing and face-washing that seemed to go on there night and day.

This was not the cause of his silence and abstraction, however, any more than it was the cause of his excessive smoking.

He smoked more than two ounces every day. "It's because he's not on rations here," suggested the suspicious world. But it was wrong, as it so often is. The real reason for Hookey's manners and customs was that he had a great deal of thinking to do, and he found that ideas always made their way to his brain most easily through the shank of his pipe.

His thinking was really finished on the second last

evening of his visit. But he was not the man to give away the results of his thought at an inauspicious moment; so he smoked away all the last day of his visit. The *Arica* was to sail the next afternoon; so Ned, Campbell, Martin, and he were to set out early next morning for Liverpool, where the vessel was berthed.

As their last night ashore was closing in, they all gathered round the fire in the smoking-room before dinner, and nobody seemed to have any desire to talk. This was the chance Hookey had been waiting for. His words were not likely to be thrown away here; so he removed his long clay from his lips, and remarked in a casual way,—

"Moles is wot I calls 'em—*moles.*"

Ned had been expecting something for a while, but he feigned great surprise, and asked—just as he knew the old fellow expected him to ask—

"Who's moles, Hookey? Or are you only talking in your sleep?"

"'Oo's moles, yer askin'? Ye'd better ask 'oo ain't moles. Y're all moles, those o' ye 'oo ain't bats."

"Come now, Hookey, what millstone have you been spying through this time?" said Wallace sarcastically.

"Never mind him; he's jealous," struck in Ned, who was anxious for the old man's yarn, and saw chances of its being cut short. He saw that Hookey was in the yarning vein. "Now, what have you seen, eh?"

"'Tain't wot I've see'd as is 'xtraor'nary; it's wot you fellows 'a missed."

"Comes to the same thing whichever way you take it, don't it? Now, what is it?"

"That archæoly man's a knowin' sort, an' knows more'n most. I'm astonished 'e didn' see't. But then 'e's not a seafarin' man, an' 'e's to be excused. But t'others—humph!"

"If you don't speak up, I'm going to run my scarf-pin into you. That's one good thing of having a real gold pin: it only hurts; it never poisons."

This obviously had an effect on Hookey. He knew that Campbell had a habit of carrying out his threats.

"It's this 'ere business o' the treasure an' them skulls an' skeletons. Nobody seems to 'a guessed the truth."

"And what is the truth, you who know it?"

"Well, there's a lot o' truth, an' I'm not sayin' as I've got it all pat, but it seems to me 'as it 'angs middlin' well together. O' course I wasn't there to see the things 'appen. But maybe I'd better spin't off as I think it did 'appen, by way o' a yarn like—founded on fac', as the story-books says."

"That's your ticket, Hookey. Stick to yarning; it's more in your line than history."

Paying no attention to Wallace's sneer, Hookey took up his tale.

CHAPTER XVIII.

OLD HOOKEY EXPLAINS.

"'BOUT the en' o' the year 1554, the queen's 'eadsman 'ad a dirty job on. He'd to cut the 'eads off' two brothers called Sir Walter Campadder an' Arthur Campadder. He was middlin' used to cuttin' off' 'eads, was this 'eadsman, but some'ow 'e didn' like this job. Fur, ye see, both o' the brothers was middlin' good fighters, an' 'ad given it 'ot to the Dons; an' though 'e was a Papist, this 'ere 'eadsman was a Englishman more, an' didn' like to do away wi' two fine fightin' men, and 'em likely to be needin' fighters soon.

"But business is business, an' the 'eadsman was gettin' ready to cut into the Campadders, w'en the man as 'ad charge o' the 'ead-cuttin' departmen'—a mean skunk 'at answered to the name o' Hugh Fitzashby—comes up, an' sez 'e to the 'eadsman, sez 'e,—

"'It's a pity to waste a good 'ead w'en it may turn out wuth somethin'.'

"'W'ich o' them 'eads 'as a markit vally?' sez the 'eadsman.

"'Oh, Sir Walter's,' sez Hugh.

"''Ow much?' sez the 'eadsman.

"'That depen's,' sez Hugh. 'Maybe a hunner crowns, maybe five hunner.'

"''Ow much is it wuth to-day?' asks the 'eadsman.

"'A hunner, an' the rest if the 'ead turns out a good investmen'.'

"''Eads is up to-day,' sez the 'eadsman. 'Make it two hunner down, an' five hunner more if 'eads is trumps, an' then I'll maybe deal.'

"'Done!' sez Hugh; 'an' promotion fur you, besides, if't all comes right. But 'ow're we goin' to manage? We must show two 'eads to the inspector o' 'eads w'en he comes roun'. Maybe we could square 'im, but I don' want so many in the swim.'

"But the 'eadsman jus' winked, and sed 'e knew 'is way about among 'eads. Ye see at that time the 'ead business was partic'lar lively, an' it 'ad two branches— a public branch an' a privit. The public 'eads was well looked into, an' no capers could be tried on 'em. They 'ad all to be stuck on poles an' h'isted above the

Tower o' Lunnon, if they wasn' sent a-starrin' i' the provinces, to show they was reely dead. But the privit ones didn' matter much, so long's the 'eadsman's list tallied wi' th' inspector's.

"'There's Sir Willimet in Nummer 13. 'Is 'ead was promised to Sir Linsel, 'oo 'ad 'im put in very privit, an' nobody knows as Sir Willimet's 'ere at all. An' now Sir Linsel's own 'ead is due to-day, at the fust round, an' then ye see I've a 'ead to spare, an' no questions asked. I've of'en a spare 'ead like that. Sometimes I sells the 'ead to itsel', and sometimes to somebody else; it all depen's on 'oo 'as mos' money. Some 'eads is shameful poor, an' the queer thing is 'at the poores' 'eads is of'en the deares' to buy fro' the outside. I can easy nip off Sir Willimet's 'ead—it's a cheap un at best—an' pass it on along o' Arthur's. The inspector'll never know the difference.'"

"You bloodthirsty ruffian!" broke out Wallace, shrinking from the old sailor with a dramatic drawing away of his jacket from contamination. But the others resented the interruption, and Hookey was soon on his way again.

"So Hugh got Sir Walter out o' the 'ead departmen', an' 'ad 'im smuggled away to a castle o' 'is own, w'ere 'e saved 'im up to see if 'e would turn out to be wuth keepin'. The castle was called Scranlet Castle. It isn't far fro' the abbey itsel'; an' if ye want to know more about it, old Patter—what-ye-may-call-'im—'ll tell ye all ye want to know about it, an' a deal more.

"So Sir Walter was kep' there warm an' comfortable, an' 'ad good feedin', till Hugh saw 'ow the treasure-'unt would come on. Fur 'e 'ad a good idea, 'ad Hugh, 'at the map was all my eye; and then, if the treasure was still to be looked for, 'e'd an idea 'at 'e'd sort o' 'a the bulge on the queen's men now. They allus was too 'andy wi' their 'ead-cuttin' at that time. No wunner they called 'er Bloody Mary.

"Well, it turns out all jus' as Hugh 'ad supposed. The queen's men came back wi'out the treasure, an' then Hugh thought 'twas time to take a look in at 'is castle o' Scranlet, an' see wot Sir Walter 'ad to say on the subjec'. He tried to pump Sir Walter; but Sir Walter 'ad more sense. Hugh offered to go 'alves wi' 'im, an' set 'im free besides; but Sir Walter knew a trick wuth two o' that.

"So Hugh tried a new dodge. He put 'im into a dark cell, an' chained 'im agin the wall, so 'e could neither sit nor stan', an' gen'r'lly made things uncomfortable fur 'im. But 'e gave 'im enough to eat, for 'e didn' want 'im to die on 'is 'an's.

"All this time 'at Hugh was a-cheatin' o' the gover'men', 'e was a-curryin' favour wi' the queen's men; an' as a rewar' o' 'is faithful services, 'e 'ad got a gran' o' the abbey an' lan's o' Arnwyke.

"But 'e didn' want to show 'is paper yet, fur 'e 'ad an idea 'at maybe some o' the Campadders as was loose knew summat about the treasure; an' 'e wanted to give 'em rope, so's 'e could keep an eye on 'em all the time 'e was a-workin' up Sir Walter.

"At last Sir Walter got sick o' bein' chained up like a dog in a 'ole, an' made up 'is min' to tell 'is secret an' take 'is chance. He'd little 'ope o' gettin' the treasure, but 'e thought 'e might get away some'ow if on'y 'e was aboar' a boat agin. Likely 'e wanted to see the wa'er again before 'e died. No seafarin' man likes to die in a 'ole, an' maybe Sir Walter wanted to drown 'isself decent, like a sailor man.

"So 'e sez 'e'd pilot Hugh's ship to the place w'ere the treasure was, an' then, afore the treasure was dug out, 'e was to get a boat fro' Hugh, an' a lugsail an' provisions, an' was to 'ave a chance fur 'is life.

"Hugh agreed to all this, an' so Sir Walter knew 'e meant to cheat; for nobody'd agree to let a man off afore the treasure was discovered.

"But, all the same, Sir Walter came out o' the

prison, an' was led to the shore at night, an' then put on Hugh's ship, the *Red Leper*,* an' sailed away roun' to Arnwyke.

"W'en 'e was near the shore, wi' a fine breeze over the counter a-fillin' 'er big square sails, 'e put 'er 'ead right fur the shore an' the rocks.

"'No, ye don't,' sez Hugh, angry like. 'I've kep' a eye on you all the time, suspeckin' summat o' this kin'; an' if ye try't agin, we'll 'a up the rack on deck 'ere, an' see 'ow ye like that.'

"Fur they 'ad kep' a eye on 'im, an' 'e'd 'ad no chance to slip over the bul'arks. But 'e ups, an' sez 'e knew wot 'e was about, an' the shore was all right. An' by-an'-by they began to believe 'im, an' sent out a boat; an' there, sure 'nough, was a entrance up a narrow creek into a wide gulf w'ere there was room 'nough for a bigger ship nor the *Red Leper*. So they crep' close up to the shore w'ere there was lots o' wa'er, an' they warped themselves into the gulf, an' was mighty glad to be out o' sight o' the open sea; fur it's a exposed place there, an' w'en ye're huntin' fur treasure, ye don't want company.

"Sir Hugh was quite pleasant like, fur everythin' looked uncommon like treasure in this comfortable gulf.

* *Leopard* is probably what Old Hookey meant.

"Then Sir Walter he sez, 'Gi' me my provisions an my boat now.'

"'All in good time, my 'earty,' sez Hugh. 'I gives ye my word o' 'onner ye'll get away safe an' soun' soon's the treasure's aboar'.'

"Sir Walter smiled at the 'onner o' a man like Hugh, but 'e sez nothin', an' then draws the plan o' the cave an' the gall'ry 'at ye've all seen. He said it was better'n goin' wi' the men into the cave; 'e wasn' goin' to do that. He couldn' stan' that, 'e sez— seein' all 'is treasure pirited like that.

"Hugh didn' want 'im partic'lar in the cave; wot 'e wanted was the treasure, an' it looked as if 'e'd got it this time, at last. But bein' a careful man, 'e sent some o' 'is sailors fust up the stairs into the gall'ry an' into the cave. An' everythin' was jus' as Sir Walter 'ad said it was, an' the gall'ry went to the right place.

"So w'en 'e knowed there was no danger, Hugh went 'imself, an' he made fust for Nummer 1, jus' as Sir Walter 'ad told 'em to. An' they 'ad the secret o' the way o' openin' the stone coffins wi' the iron boxes inside, an' all they'd to do was to get the iron boxes aboar'.

"It took a lot o' time an' a peck o' trouble afore

the fust box was got aboar'; an' then they opened it, an' saw all the gold an' precious stones an' rubies an' sich. An' then Sir Walter wanted 'is boat.

"At first Hugh thought 'e'd let 'im 'ave the boat, an' 'ave done wi' 'im. But then 'e thought it was allus safer not to 'ave enemies runnin' about the seas, especially fighters like Sir Walter. So 'e sez,—

"' 'Old on, can't yer, till we've got the 'ole thing aboar'; there'll be time 'nough then, an' it looks like win' now any'ow.'

"W'en the next box was h'isted aboar', Sir Walter agin asked fur 'is boat, an' was agin put off.

"' 'Ow do we know the others ain't dummies?' sneered Hugh. 'You just wait peaceable like till we've got the 'ole thing aboar'.'

"' But the next box, Nummer 3, is the biggest an' richest box o' the lot—it's no dummy. Wait till ye see wot it's like, afore ye talk o' treasure.'

"But this made Hugh think. He was near out o' his skin wi' joy a'ready, an' 'e began to think it might be dangerous if 'is men got an idea o' 'ow much 'e was wuth now. Ye see 'e was afraid o' 'is own men a'ready. Pirits allus is w'en prizes is about. So 'e thought 'e'd not take 'is men this time, in case they'd see this preciousest chest.

"He wasn't quite sure at first; but w'en 'e see'd 'at Sir Walter wanted 'im to take lots o' men wi' 'im, 'e soon made up 'is min' not to take nobody but 'is own son, an' one o' the gunners to open the lock.

"'But it's far heavier nor the other uns,' sez Sir Walter.

"'All right,' sez Hugh—'we'll manage all right; we knows our way about among treasures.'

"'Please yersel',' sez Sir Walter; 'but ye'll be sorry fur't.'

"My idea is 'at Sir Walter wanted to get a great lot o' the Red Lepers ashore, an' then 'e'd offer to share all the treasure they 'ad aboar' wi' 'em as was left behin', if they'd make 'im cap'n; an' then they'd sail off wi' the *Red Leper* to the Spanish Main, an' make more fortunes. Anyway 'e didn' get the chance. Fur Hugh took on'y 'is son an' the gunner an' the 'eadsman; fur, by-the-bye, I furgot to tell ye 'at Hugh 'ad kep' 'is word to the 'eadsman, an' 'ad took 'im wi' 'im in the *Red Leper*, an' 'ad made 'im second mate. The 'eadsman thought it was promotion, but my idea is 'at Hugh on'y wanted to keep the fellow near 'im, so's 'e wouldn' tell no tales; an' then w'en the treasure was foun', it would be time to promote 'im to a steady job wi' Davy Jones.

"So the four o' 'em mounts the steps, an' the 'eadsman was told off to do sentry-go at the corner w'ere the gall'ry turns roun', an' t'others went on.

"The same dodge was worked fur the stone top, an' it opened quite good-natured. But the rest was none so easy. Hugh's plan was to get the box open, an' carry off all the preciousest things in bags to the ship on the sly, an' tell the men 'at there wasn' no more treasure. Likely as not the ole ruffian 'ad agreed to gi' 'is men a share o' the treasure, an' 'e'd save a lot o' shares if 'e cheated like this.

"But the gunner 'e didn' seem to catch the right way o' that lock. 'Twasn' the same's the rest. They opened quite easy like. So Hugh slips in Sir Walter's drawin' into the iron case wi' the title to 'is estate, an' shoved 'em in the inside o' 'is breastplate, an' then was goin' to help the gunner.

"Ye see pirits like Hugh never trusts nobody, so they've allus to carry all their papers an' things wi' 'em w'erever they go.

"An' jus' as Hugh was makin' to go to 'elp the gunner, the lock started its capers, an' blew them all into kingdom come—partic'larly the gunner, 'oo only left the little bone the doctor foun'!

"All this time Sir Walter was a-walkin' up an' down the quarter-deck o' the *Red Leper* wi' Hugh's third mate, tryin' to persuade 'im to join in wi' 'im an' seize the ship. The mate was middlin' willin', fur 'e 'ated Hugh. But 'e sed it was no good so long's the firs' mate was there. Then 'e tells Sir Walter, privit like, 'at this firs' mate 'ad a'ready made arrangements on 'is own 'ook fur seizin' the ship an' throwin' Hugh overboar' as soon's all the treasure was aboar'.

"W'en Sir Walter 'eard this, 'e went for'ard to w'ere the firs' mate was, an' meant to chuck the treacherous fellow over the side, w'en all at once the thunner o' the explosion put a stop to everythin'.

"W'en the smoke comes a-pourin' out o' the gall'ry w'ere the steps was, every man jack aboar' the *Red Leper* gets into a funk; fur the 'igh rocks all roun' were rattlin' away wi' the echoes as if the 'ole place wos a-tumblin' about their ears.

"'Soon's some o' the brave uns came to their senses, they wanted to land and go up the gall'ry to see wot 'ad 'appened. 'Twas on'y the brave uns 'at wanted this; the rest wanted to lay 'ands on Sir Walter. But 'e wasn' to be foun' now'ere. They thought 'e'd dropped overboar', an' was swimmin' fur 'is life; so they kep' their 'eads over the bul'arks, wi' their guns i' their 'ands, ready for a pot shot.

"But Sir Walter wasn' there; 'e 'ad other business on 'and. He was down below, a-bustin' open a door. An' w'en 'e got in, 'e didn't waste any time. He laid 'old o' a gun, an' loaded it, an' then 'e did the same fur another; an' then 'e 'unted out two bits o' a soft sort o' cord, an' made two nice little slow matches. Then 'e fixed up some o' the cases o' gunpowder convenient for 'is purpose, an' put some little 'eaps o' powder 'ere an' there ready. Then 'e lights 'is matches, an' sat waitin' fur company.

"Naterally 'e 'adn' long to wait. Soon's they foun' 'e wasn' overboar', they 'ad a pretty good idea w'ere to fin' 'im.

"W'en the firs' mate gets to the door o' the magazine, 'e sings out to Sir Walter to drop that thing, or it would be worse fur 'im. Sir Walter didn' seem to see't; so the mate sings out to drop that thing, an' it would be better fur 'im. All 'at Sir Walter sez was,—

"'Sen' the third mate 'ere.'

"W'en the third mate comes, Sir Walter sings out,—

"'If ye want the *Red Leper* to last more'n quarter

o' an hour, ye'll throw this fellow overboar', after blowin' out 'is brains 'ere.'

"The firs' mate began laughin', but 'e 'ad the laugh all to 'imself. Then they began shovin' and tumblin' about, an' somebody fired a gun, an' 'it Sir Walter, an' 'e let go the match. It was very careless o' 'im. But nobody picked it up; some'ow they didn' 'ave time. Besides, w'en a lighted match falls among loose powder, it don' need to be picked up; it rises itself, an' lifts things wi' it. This match lifted the 'ole *Red Leper* an' all aboard 'er, an' made such a smash all roun' 'at the rocks came a-tumblin' down, an' covered up the 'ole o' the gulf w'ere the *Red Leper* 'ad been; an' since nobody knew about the gulf, o' course nobody missed it, an' so it lay hidden till t'other day."

* * * * *

That is Old Hookey's explanation. Ornamentation apart, it may be true; even the best of story-tellers will occasionally stumble into the truth.

THE END.

www.ingramcontent.com/pod-product-compliance
Lightning Source LLC
Chambersburg PA
CBHW030254240426
43673CB00040B/966